# GETTING JOBS
# BY GLYN
# JORDAN

http://gjbygj.blogspot.com

**Blogs Postings to Assist Individuals
in Finding Employment**

**By
Glyn Jordan**

ISBN: 1469969033
ISBN: 9781469969039

*This book is dedicated to my wife, Ann, who has devoted a great amount of time in reading, editing, and advising me. In addition, it is dedicated to individuals who are seeking satisfying and fulfilling work.*

# FOREWORD

In 1986 I went back to school to earn a PhD. The reason for this return is a story for another day. However, on this day I was thinking about a subject for my dissertation. I was listening to a radio talk show while I was returning to Dallas, where I now lived, after a visit to my hometown of Hubbard, Texas.

The program featured a guest from the Texas Employment Commission (subsequently renamed the Texas Workforce Commission) who was responsible for the commission's job search seminar program. The job search seminars were held weekly at the commission's office in Richardson, Texas, and were free for all individuals seeking employment.

Having previously been unemployed myself, I was interested in learning more about the seminar. The guest explained how the seminar had resulted in many job seekers finding employment. The next day I visited the Texas Employment Commission office in Richardson, which was the start of a series of steps that ended with my dissertation: *An Empirical Examination of Texas Employment Commission Outplacement Services.*

Here is the abstract of my dissertation:

Outplacement is a structured group of activities that assist the employee in obtaining a new position. The effectiveness of the outplacement service provided by the Texas Employment Commission, specifically the job search seminar, was studied from the perspective of job-relevant outcomes and psychological outcomes. Based on repeated measures of surveys completed by participants in job search seminars, it was shown that participants realized larger increases in self-esteem, internal locus of control, and life satisfaction than members of a control group. Using moderator regression techniques, it was shown that the length of immediate prior tenure, former earnings, level of education, and age in some cases moderate the impact of the outplacement process. Individuals with the shortest prior tenure realized the largest increase in life satisfaction. Individuals with the largest prior earnings realized the largest reduction in external locus of control. Younger individuals realized the largest increase in internal locus of control; however, older individuals realized larger reduction in external locus of control. A job search index was developed that served as an independent variable representing the increase in job search knowledge gained over the quasi-experiment period. (Jordan, *An Empirical Examination of Texas Employment Commission Outplacement Services*, 1990)

The experience I gained from this study made a lasting impression on me. I recognized the importance for out-of-work individuals to learn the necessary job search skills to assist them in becoming reemployed. Since my graduation, I have devoted much of my time in assisting individuals finding employment. It is to this end that I continue to develop my blog, Getting Jobs by Glyn Jordan.

# CONTENTS

# SECTION 1 – INTRODUCTION

In early August 2009, my wife and I went to see *Julie & Julia*, a movie about how Julia Child entered the cooking profession, which then intertwined with blogger Julie Powell's cooking experiences. In 1963 Child began her television cooking show. Julie wanted to re-create all of Child's signature recipes, so she developed a blog in which she daily described her efforts to cook one. As described in the movie, Julie's blog became quite a sensation, attracting many avid followers.

After the movie, I began to think about developing my own blog that would provide advice and assistance to job seekers. That very afternoon I went home, got on the Internet, and found that I could establish a blog on Google for no cost. The result was the blog *Getting Jobs by Glyn Jordan,* which was first posted on August 10, 2009. The stated purpose of the blog is:

This blog contains information for job seekers. Job search experiences of Glyn Jordan are included as comments. The purpose of the blog is to contain information for job seekers. My own experiences are included as comments, and readers are encouraged to share their own job search experiences with others. All job search suggestions are welcomed.

After posting over 200 entries in the blog, I have decided to compile a book that categorizes and groups the individual blog postings by job search topic. The time and energy that I have devoted to this project have been rewarding to me. Perhaps my effort in itself can be an example to job seekers illustrating how success follows dedicated effort and focus.

The first blogs of Getting Jobs by Glyn Jordan are contained in Appendix B.

# SECTION II – OBJECTIVES AND RÉSUMÉS

Because the blogs have been written over a two-year period, some of the information may seem dated; however, I have tried to remove materials that are no longer relevant to job seeking today. In subsequent versions of this book, I plan to add new posts and remove older ones.

A cliché that I frequently use in my MBA courses at the University of Phoenix is that if you do not know where you are going, any road will get your there! Another one is that if you do not know where you are going, how will you know when you arrive? As discussed in blog posts in this section, it is important that job seekers take time to determine their short- and long-range objectives. I understand, however, if one needs a job, then any job offered is welcomed. Another one of my clichés is that if it is raining, any shelter will do. However, employers understand this situation, and that is why so many applicants hear the term "overqualified."

Following are this section's compilation of blog posts:

# Do You Have a Personal Strategic Plan?

I have been teaching strategic management courses in MBA programs in several universities in the Dallas–Fort Worth Metroplex and online for many years. I often ask my students if they have a strategic plan. In most cases the answer is, "I have a plan, but it is not documented."

For readers who have taken business classes, the acronym SWOT (strengths, weaknesses, opportunities, and threats) is a familiar term. I encourage all readers to take a blank sheet of paper, divide it into four quadrants, and label the quadrants with the SWOT terms. Next, identify and record in the appropriate quadrant at least four strengths, weaknesses, opportunities, and threats. Your task is to:

1. Identify areas of opportunities that take advantage of your strengths.

2. Identify areas of weaknesses that need to be avoided or strengthened.

3. Begin activities that will increase your strengths.

4. Begin activities that will reduce your weaknesses.

# Do You Have a Brand?

A brand is very important in marketing and is defined in the article "A New Focus in Job Searching" in the July 25, 2010, edition of *The Dallas Morning News* in section 1J. In marketing, branding is an intangible collection of perceptions in the consumer's mind about a product or service. A brand name helps to raise awareness and builds trust in a crowded marketplace. Personal branding is the process of distinguishing the essence of an individual's relevant career attributes and communicating them consistently throughout the résumé and interview process.

I think the branding concept is important and may be the key for an applicant to win a job. What are five or six keywords that represent your brand? The article suggests that you should integrate such words in your résumé and interview. The words about me that come to mind are teacher, husband, father, volunteer, salesman, and enabler.

What are the words that describe your brand?

# Take Advantage of Your Strengths and Experience

A basic task in strategic management is to develop a SWOT (strengths, weaknesses, opportunities, and threats) analysis for the organization under study. Why, you ask? Typically the mission of an organization is to survive and grow. A proven approach to success is to capitalize on strengths, minimize weaknesses (or perhaps remove them), take advantage of opportunities, and avoid threats.

I was assisting an individual at a SCORE, a volunteer organization associated with the Small Business Administration, counseling session this past week. He said that he wanted to start a business in the oil industry. Furthermore he stated that oil prices are very high and that he would like to make a lot of money. I asked the person if he had experience in oil. He said no, but perhaps someone would hire him and teach him the business. Next I asked him about his job experience, and he replied that he was fluent in three languages and was currently a bus driver.

I suggested to the client that he pursue opportunities in areas in which he could use his expertise, which was not oil. I am not saying that no oil-based organization would hire him, but his chances of finding a job involving some sort of transportation or using his gift of languages were much greater.

If you are seeking employment, I suggest that you develop your own SWOT, analyze it, and act accordingly.

# Devise a Strategy

In the December 29, 2010, edition of *The Dallas Morning News,* on page 2D, was an article by Diane Stafford of the Kansas City Star entitled "Right Job Won't Be Handed to You" that provided some strategies for job seekers. Stafford makes a good point about waiting for someone to suddenly offer you a job. Lightning does strike; however, your chances of being struck are small. So if you want a job, perhaps some of the following strategies will help:

- Use LinkedIn. Recruiters are frequent visitors of LinkedIn because they know that people who know people are the best resource.

- Don't just look to well-worn paths. After joining the crowd with online job postings, you should expand fishing locations and throw out more nets!

- Spend only a fraction of your time answering online ads—focus on specialty niches, trade publications, and corporate websites.

- Get out of the house. Attend professional and association meetings in your field.

- Don't pass up doors that don't seem to offer sufficient money or challenges. Any port in a storm provides shelter.

- Go to job clubs, community career offices at community colleges, and large public libraries. There are many sources of information for job seekers, including my blog.

- Don't masquerade as someone you're not. In a previous blog posting, I urged readers to conduct a personal SWOT analysis.

- Study the landscape. Look in areas and industries that are hiring.

- Remember your manners. Thank everyone who helps and smile a lot.

The new year will bring opportunities for us all. It is important that we follow these three Rs:

Recognize the opportunities.

Reflect on them.

React to them.

# Post Accurate, Error-Free Résumés in Open Text

An article by Metro Creative Connection in the October 4, 2009, issue of *The Dallas Morning News,* on page 1J, entitled "Landing a Job in the Digital Age," had several recommendations, including developing a personal website and using buzzwords on your site, joining and participating in social networking, and using technology.

I think that the following suggestions about technology are most helpful:

- Use standard typefaces and type sizes for your résumés. Many organizations scan documents, so fancy fonts may not be accurately scanned.

- Do not attach your résumé to your e-mail. With the concern about viruses, you should post your résumé in the body of your e-mail instead.

- Use the subject line of the e-mail to introduce yourself.

- Proofread, spell-check, and read aloud your e-mail. Errors in your e-mail could immediately eliminate you from job consideration.

I was interviewing candidates to be my secretary. After interviewing several candidates, I selected the person to receive an offer. Unfortunately, she had a typing error on her listed telephone number. Needless to say, if she could not get her own telephone number correct on her résumé, I did not want her to be my secretary.

# Job Hunter Support System

An article by Diane Stafford in *The Dallas Morning News* on March 8, 2010, on page 9A, entitled "Job Hunters Need a Support System," discussed the importance of job seekers receiving support from friends, family, and other job seekers.

If you know a job seeker who has given up trying to find a job, I encourage you to be there for him or her.

Perhaps you can provide valuable job leads or simply express your understanding and encouragement. When an individual loses hope and self-respect, nothing good happens.

# Résumé Writing for a Recession

"Résumé Writing for a Recession," an article on page 1J in the August 22, 2010, edition of *The Dallas Morning News,* credited to staff and wire reports, provided a number of suggestions for individuals seeking employment in a job market flooded with people looking for work.

One of the article's suggestions is to avoid chronological formatting in a résumé because many job seekers have gaps of employment during this period of high unemployment.

I personally think that avoiding disclosure of gaps of employment does not disguise the fact that such gaps exist. A skillful interviewer will quickly investigate the applicant's work history. The employment situation is not a secret, and the hiring organization will appreciate honesty shown by an applicant.

The article suggests that résumés should be tailored to the target employer by excluding irrelevant information and emphasizing accomplishments that fit the hiring organization's requirements.

# Reference Check

An article on page 2D in the September 29, 2010, edition of *The Dallas Morning News*, "Reference Check," by Diane Stafford of the *Kansas City Star,* provided some important suggestions concerning one's references. References are very important, particularly for individuals who have been out of the workplace for some time. Here are the suggestions:

- Don't list references from more than ten years ago. What these people say may not be relevant today.

- A good reference doesn't have to be a boss. A peer who has a good reputation or high profile in the profession is equally valuable.

- If past bosses aren't available, consider using vendors or clients.

- Have you been an active volunteer? The executive director of the nonprofit could comment on your energy, dependability, and attitude.

- Professors and teachers can vouch for communication skills, the ability to meet deadlines, and overall intelligence.

- Religious leaders can speak to character.

It is important to obtain approval from your references. In addition, I think that you should discuss what they would comment about you to an inquiring party.

Your references should be current and well-informed about the kind of job you are seeking and able to speak accurately about your credentials.

You should assume that your references will be contacted. Once I interviewed an individual for a computer programming position. He gave me the contact information for his previous boss as his reference. I called the reference, who immediately informed me that the applicant was not dependable and should not be hired. Needless to say, I wished the applicant Godspeed.

# Keywords and Online Résumés

"Treat Your Job Search Like a Job," an article by Cliff Garinn on page 1J in the August 29, 2010, edition of *The Dallas Morning News*, discussed online programs that employers use to "weed out those who don't fit the qualifications or who cannot follow instructions."

I suggest that you tailor your résumé for each potential employer. Insert words in your résumé that are used in the organization's advertisement. If the organization is seeking an outside salesperson and you have relevant experience, you should mention the term *outside sales* in your résumé. Further, you need to follow the instructions from the organization to the letter! Creative writing and discussion of unrelated experience should be avoided.

I have noticed that Google is able to post job ads in my blog based on the subject of the blog. For example, I suggested that job seekers consider getting alternative certification in order to get a teaching job, and Google posted ads in my blog from organizations providing alternative certification classes.

Finally, proofread your e-mail prior to submission. I develop my postings using Word's editing and spelling features; unfortunately, I still find errors. My old saying is that the best way to proof a document is to publish it and the readers will find your errors!

# Tailor Résumés to Fit the Job

An article on page 1J in *The Dallas Morning News* on June 6, 2010, entitled "Tailor Résumé to Fit the Job," by Cliff Garinn, discussed ideas concerning your résumé. Here are some of the suggestions:

- Employers do not want to figure out or interpret what your skills are and how they relate to their needs. You should, therefore, develop a résumé that answers the question: What can I do for the hiring organization?

- Employers are not proofreaders; consequently, your résumé should be error free, concise, and easy to read.

- The one-size-fits-all résumé is not a good idea. You should tailor your résumé for your target audience—the hiring organization.

The article suggests that you include only the past ten years of experience in your résumé. I do not agree; you may have relevant experience that occurred some time ago. Of course, I am a bit long in the tooth and am pleased with some of my earlier days in my career.

You should list only completed academic accomplishments beyond high school.

Memberships in professional organizations, if they are relevant to the organization's focus, should be included.

Hobbies typically are of no interest to the hiring organization unless they are in some way work-related.

# Treat Job Search as a Full-Time Job

Section J of the August 23, 2009, edition of *The Dallas Morning News* had an article by Metro Creative Connection entitled "Treat the Job Search as a Full-Time Job." Here are some of its suggestions for your job search:

1. Target your search. Narrow your search by focusing on jobs that most interest you by making a list of organizations that have such jobs even if there are no current job openings.

2. Sell yourself. You need to be able to discuss why an organization should hire you in terms of results you can produce.

3. Focus on growth or recession-proof industries. An Internet search will assist in identifying such industries.

4. Emphasize results, not skills. It is important to highlight prior accomplishments rather than specific skills.

5. Make it personal. Do your homework on target organizations and customize your résumé and discussions in job interviews accordingly.

6. Money talks. An old saying is that the first person to mention money loses. It is a good idea to keep an open mind on money topics.

7. Stay positive and flexible. Keep looking when nothing seems to develop. One option is to consider freelance or contract work while continuing your search.

# Why Did Jesse James Rob Banks?

During my wife's and my visit to Nova Scotia, Prince Edward Island, and New Brunswick, we frequently heard locals say the reason why the population in their provinces is declining is the lack of opportunities for young people. Such conversations remind me of the old saying about Jesse James: "Why do you rob banks, Jesse?" "It is because that is where the money is!"

I do not blame anyone for moving to find meaningful and productive work. Such moves frequently require sacrifices by individuals seeking opportunities; however, reluctance to make changes may deprive individuals of a better life.

Horace Greeley is often credited with a famous quote actually made by John B. L. Soule. The quote first appeared as the title to an 1851 *Terre Haute Express* editorial written by Soule. Along with being wrongly credited to Greeley, it has also often been misquoted. It was originally written as:

"Go West, young man, and grow up with the country."

This information is quoted from an editorial by David Chuhran posted on the Internet.

I think that the message is for job seekers to consider relocating where the job opportunities exist even it means moving west, north, east, or south!

# 12 Myths to Trash If You Want to Get Hired

No matter what career you're seeking, finding employment continues to be a challenge. To improve your chances, avoid these common misconceptions, career experts advise (posted by USAA, www.usaa.com).

Myth 1: Most jobs are advertised in newspapers and online sites.

Only 15 percent to 20 percent of job openings are publicly posted, reports Randall Hansen, publisher of Quintessential Careers website. The number of people actually hired through these ads is less than half that, he says.

To add insult to unemployment, many employers have increasingly found e-job applications more of a hassle than a help, says Christine Bolzan, founder of Graduate Career Coaching. "So many people automatically respond to the online offerings that employers are often reluctant to post a job," she says.

If you search online for a job, Hansen recommends going directly to prospective employers' websites or searching

Google by profession, industry, or geographic area. "Many industry and professional associations also run job boards," he says. "For example, the American Marketing Association has one for marketing professionals."

Myth 2: The web is the modern way to search for work.

Use the Internet to gather information and promote yourself, but don't depend on it as a one-stop e-shop for good job opportunities. Instead, focus on getting real face time. "Person-to-person networking has never been more important," says Bolzan, who offers these suggestions to advertise yourself:

- Sound out friends and family about openings.

- Schedule informational interviews with people in your field of interest.

- Catch up with former colleagues and classmates.

- Get involved in professional organizations.

Myth 3: Résumé + cover letter = interview ± job.

Today, you have to market yourself and your skills, says J. T. O'Donnell, a career strategist and founder of Careerealism.com. Consider a career-focused website or blog as a way to tell your story, she says.

Use professional networking sites like LinkedIn to promote your experience, research what's current in your career field, and develop professional contacts.

Myth 4: The more applications in play, the more offers on the way.

Put away the application shotgun and become a job sharpshooter, advises O'Donnell. Study the positions you want and identify the companies that have them. Then, aim carefully by crafting customized résumés and cover letters designed to hit the mark. "It's a matter of quality over quantity," she says.

Myth 5: Any job in this economy is a good job.

If the rent is due and your desired line of work still eludes you, taking a career detour may be unavoidable. At the same time, keep faith with your long-range professional goals and keep your skills current by staying active in related organizations, taking a class to add new skills, or volunteering for an organization that relates to the job you're interested in.

Myth 6: Experience and qualifications matter more than character.

Most interviewers gauge how well candidates might fit in with their team. At your interview, smile, make eye contact, ask informed questions, and demonstrate genuine enthusiasm for the position. Never undervalue authenticity and likability in your effort to win the job, advises O'Donnell.

Myth 7: It's not what you know; it's whom you know.

It's more a matter of how well you know them, when you knew them, and whom they know, says Bolzan. "You need to stay in contact with decision makers even when they aren't hiring," she adds. "You need to let them know you're still out there by gently touching base every thirty to forty-five days."

Myth 8: The interview is all about you.

A job interview is more than a one-way audition of your skills and personality. You also need to show genuine interest in the company and position.

Learn everything you can about the company and the person who will be interviewing you, if you can find out that person's name. Scope out online information about the company through Google searches. Learn about your interviewer through LinkedIn company profiles and corporate tweeters. Shared alma maters, favorite teams, or professional memberships can go a long way to breaking the interview ice.

Myth 9: Dumbing down your résumé is an effective strategy.

If you've been told you're overqualified, you might be tempted to remove dates and even advanced degrees from your résumé. This would be a mistake, says O'Donnell. Such a move smacks of desperation and can be a deal killer if a background check reveals the truth.

A better approach is to explain in detail why you're enthusiastic about the position and the company and what specific needs you are uniquely qualified to meet. Also, demonstrate you have the flexibility and qualities to mesh with the team. Ask questions and show your readiness to learn what others have to teach.

Myth 10: Grad school is not always a good fallback.

"Only go to grad school if you can 100 percent prove that you need those skills to advance your long-term goals," says O'Donnell. Using higher education as a place to wait out a down job market could leave you further behind financially and professionally.

Myth 11: Landing a job you love is the most important thing.

Instead of fixating on your vision of the ideal job, concentrate on how you like to live, learn, and relate. Ask yourself:

- Do you prefer to work solo, or as part of a team?

- Do you thrive in high-pressure situations, or easy-going environments?

- Is your computer like an extension of your fingers and brain, or a necessary electronic evil?

Leverage this self-knowledge to target jobs and careers that play to these preferences and strengths. The resulting job might not be perfect, but if you are tackling tasks you enjoy on a daily basis, you might end up with the next best thing.

Myth 12: If you've been fired, your job prospects are toast.

Getting fired or laid off doesn't carry the stigma it once did. What counts is how you handle interview questions about the situation. Whatever you do, don't rip into your old boss or workplace. Take the rational, philosophical route. Think of jobs like shoes—some fit better than others. You can use that analogy when discussing lost jobs, says O'Donnell. "Tell the interviewer, 'It just wasn't a good fit.'" Then, finish that thought by explaining why this job seems tailor-made.

# Valuable Job Search Tips

*The Dallas Morning News* in an article on page 1J in its January 24, 2010, issue, "How to Find Valuable Employees," by Bulletin Board and edited by Amy Winter, listed the following tips for job seekers and employees who want to be team players:

- A winning mind-set – Workers should have an optimistic and realistic attitude.

- Quickness on their feet – How will you as a job seeker deal with an unhappy customer?

- An eye on the prize – What process is used to make a difficult decision?

- Good sportsmanship – Integrity and truthfulness are essential to an organization's success.

- Stay optimistic – Accentuate the positive!

- Join a social networking site – A job seeker should consider joining LinkedIn, Facebook, or Twitter.

- Attend a professional/trade association meeting – Meetings provide important networking opportunities.

- Ask for more duties – One should welcome opportunities to shine!

- Join a workplace committee – One should volunteer time to serve others.

- Look at an organization's goals and compare them with your goals – Will this employer be a good fit?

- Find ways to reduce costs – Cost-saving ideas voiced in an interview may impress the interviewer.

# Finding Work

An article posted on the Internet by Metro Creative Connection, "Finding Work in a Still-Struggling Economy," provides the following steps job seekers can take to increase chances of finding a fulfilling career:

1. Make a daily commitment. Finding a job is a full-time job, so a daily schedule devoted to finding work is essential.

2. Don't sit on leads. Time is of the essence, so react immediately to job leads. You are not the only one seeking employment.

3. Tailor letters to each specific job. A form-appearing letter may end up in a round file. Develop each letter to a specific job, explaining how your individual skills match the open position.

4. Network with friends, family, and past colleagues. Many people are out of work, so you should not be ashamed to be unemployed. Many employed people are employed today only because they networked and it paid off.

5. Don't be caught off guard. Job openings don't last very long, and the applicant who's ready to jump on a job opening is the one who's most likely to land the job.

# Have You Stopped Looking for a Job?

I am thinking that many job seekers are discouraged and have stopped looking for a job. An article entitled "Have You Stopped Looking for a Job?" in the February 7, 2010, issue of *The Dallas Morning News* suggested that the sooner you work through your feelings, the sooner you will be back to work—somewhere!

You may be spending too much time looking back with regret; however, your future job is not in your past!

I suggest that you spend some time listing your strengths and mapping your strengths to organizations that can take advantage of them.

Further, once such organizations have been identified, you should activate a strategy to get in front of their hiring managers.

# How We're Making It Work

The *Parade* magazine insert in the April 11, 2010, issue of *The Dallas Morning News* contained a wealth of advice for job seekers. "How We're Making It Work" on page 4 by George Anders described with examples how Americans are inventing new strategies to weather the recession.

For example, when Marybeth Purvis's property-sales job was eliminated, she dodged unemployment by becoming a community college teacher.

Here are some key points made in the article:

1. Developing new skills: To improve their job prospects, millions of people are heading back to school for more training.

2. Finding "safe" jobs: Education and health care added about 320,000 jobs in the past twelve months.

3. Hunkering down: Many are tightening family budgets, renegotiating mortgages, and reducing expenses such as satellite TV.

4. Working part time: More than twenty-six million people are working part time. I teach courses at the University of Phoenix.

5. Starting a business: Each year 500,000 Americans start their own businesses.

As a volunteer for SCORE, Counselors for Small Business, I encourage you to visit our website, www. score.org, and call for an appointment to meet and discuss your ideas with an experienced counselor for free!

# Stay Focused During Lazy Days of Summer

"Stay Focused During Lazy Days of Summer," an article on page 1J in the August 1, 2010, edition of *The Dallas Morning News*, provided a summary of Tom Hall's book *How to Use Key Core Strategies to Grow Your Business*. I think that the following ideas Hall provided are helpful for job seekers:

- Concentrate on your strategy to get meaningful employment by producing a to-do list.

- Update the list with responsibilities and cross out completed items.

- Vacation doesn't mean you avoid job search activities. While on vacation, do not forget about deadlines and contacting individuals in your job search network.

- Maintain monitoring of all submitted job applications.

In addition, take some time to relax and recharge your job search batteries.

# Education and Job Search

*The Dallas Morning News,* in "Education Evolves to Meet Workforce Needs," an article by North American Syndicate on page 1J in the January 17, 2010, issue, quoted the following Department of Labor statistics concerning job growth over the next five years:

- Ninety percent of the fastest-growing jobs require some form of secondary education.

- There will be a 54 percent increase in information technology positions.

- There will be a 41 percent increase in veterinary technicians.

- There will be a 34 percent increase in medical assistants.

- There will be a 32 percent increase for pharmacy technicians.

- There will be a 29 percent increase in dental assistants.

- There will be a 22 percent increase for paralegals.

These statistics focus on the growing need for an educated workforce. The article encourages busy adults to consider education programs that accommodate their lifestyle. For example, there are many night classes and online classes available throughout the United States. I earned an MBA and PhD by going to night school and working full time.

# Cover Letters and Résumés

*The Dallas Morning News's* February 27, 2011, edition had an article by Cliff Garinn on page 1J discussing cover letters and résumés.

Garinn noted that your cover letter must have the look and tone of a professionally constructed letter. Obviously, the letter must be free of grammar and typographical errors, and it should also address how your skills and experience meet the organization's requirements.

If you are posting your résumé on an Internet job site, typically no cover letter is required. However, after a job interview with a prospective employer, a thank you letter is a must!

# What Types of Jobs Should You Seek!?

An article on page 1J in the May 8, 2011, edition of *The Dallas Morning News*, "A Good Fit Is a Must," by Cheryl Butler, asks what are the hot jobs for the future.

I agree with Butler that this is the wrong question for job seekers to ask. The right question is what are your strengths and interests, so you can direct your search to focus on growth industries that need your capabilities.

Just because your interest and experience may be in public relations, you do not have to restrict your search to PR firms. Almost all organizations need individuals with public relations skills. If your interests lie in accounting or administration, all growing organizations need such skills.

The article states that an individual will spend as much as 80,000 hours working over his or her lifetime. That is too much time if you are spending it doing something of only minor interest. Do the words *bored*, *uninteresting*, and *it's just a job* come to mind?

I am thinking that if you find an opportunity that contains tasks that are your passion in life, you will do a great job and will be much more satisfied and happier than if you're just doing a job that pays the rent. You probably will find that promotions and more money also follow.

# Survive and Thrive!

An article on page 1J of the May 22, 2011, issue of *The Dallas Morning News*, "At Work Don't Just Survive – Thrive," by ARAcontent, provides suggestions about how employees can keep their jobs in times when layoffs are prevalent.

This is no time to hide at work. Eileen Habelow of Randstad Employment says, "Layoffs are forcing people to wear more hats and take on more responsibility. Because of this, many people forget about exploring new opportunities with their current organizations."

Here are some of Habelow's recommendations:

- Ask questions.

- Be alert to what is going on within the organization, and schedule time with your manager to discuss your situation. Increase your value. Improve your skills, and assist others in improving theirs.

- Be social. Habelow suggests that employees be active in social media such as LinkedIn, Twitter, and Facebook. I think you have to be careful in spending too much time with these sites, which can become addictive.

- Be innovative. Employees should welcome changes and also suggest ways to improve operations.

# Improve Your Use of Time

An article on page 1J in the June 12, 2011, issue of *The Dallas Morning News*, "Accomplish More by Doing Less," by NewsUSA, encourages job seekers to take control of their lives using the following strategies:

- Stop doing the time wasters. You need to make a close analysis of how you are using your time. Planning aids such as a Day-Timer can be helpful. We tend to spend more time doing what we enjoy (perhaps watching television) than productive tasks directed toward a job search.

- Put a junk filter on your life, and just say no. Frequently, individuals receive requests to do this and that. It is easy to become overscheduled, which may result in your neglecting higher-priority tasks involving job search activities.

- Learn to delegate and to ask for help. My experience is that many individuals are willing and able to help you. I suggest that you ask for assistance in finding a job and focus on networking.

I am convinced that focused, high-energy attention to a job search will yield positive results in the form of potential job opportunities.

# Do You Pump Gasoline?

My wife, Ann, and I had a wonderful twelve-day trip to Oregon. We drove over 1,500 miles in our Hertz Toyota Yaris, which averaged over forty-one miles per gallon of gasoline! Oregon produces many agricultural products, including wheat, oats, corn, peaches, vegetables, mint, cherries, and others we were unable to identify. Timber is also a major product.

I asked our hop-a-bus tour driver in Portland about employment. He said unemployment was very high and many job seekers had become discouraged. He was a private commercial pilot who could not find a job flying and became a builder. When the doors on building jobs closed, he opened a new one and became a tour guide.

I quickly learned that I was not permitted to pump my own gasoline in Oregon. The attendants say that they appreciated having a job. So I am wondering if Oregon and many other states and cities have the right idea about self-service gasoline stations.

How do you feel about prohibiting self-service gasoline stations? I have always been in the productivity field of information systems, but there are valid arguments supporting the requirement for attendants to pump gasoline. Safety and providing preventative and required auto maintenance, which drivers often ignore, are compelling reasons.

# Jobs Opportunities in North Dakota!

Recently I become aware of the many job opportunities in North Dakota, which are primarily because of developments in the oil industry. An article in the September 18, 2011, edition of the *Wall Street Journal* on page C1, "There Will Be Oil," includes the following statement:

"In 2003, the Bakken formation in North Dakota was producing a mere 10,000 barrels of oil a day. Today, it is over 400,000 barrels, and North Dakota has become the fourth-largest oil-producing state in the country. Such 'tight' oil could add as much as two million barrels a day to the U.S. oil production after 2020—something that would not have been in any forecast five years ago."

Another article in same edition of the *Wall Street Journal,* "State Jobless Rates Climb As Governments Pare Back," states: "North Dakota has the lowest unemployment rate in the nation—3.5%—thanks to a small population and booming industries tied to natural resources. Nebraska and South Dakota also have rates below 5%."

At dinner with some friends, I asked my friend, who is purchasing oil leases in North Dakota, about the economic climate there, and he confirmed the boom is well under way. He also cautioned about the approaching cold weather season, which will slow things down a bit. A cursory review of job postings on the Internet finds many job opportunities.

I recognize that many folks do not want to leave the comfort of their present surroundings; however, if you need and want a job or you have to go to work, I suggest that you consider investigating employment opportunities in North Dakota.

# Ideas to Improve Your Résumé

An article by Cliff Garinn on page 1J in *The Dallas Morning News's* November 6, 2011, issue, "7 Tips to Strengthen Your Résumé," lists ideas that strengthen résumés.

I think that an important point to remember is that a résumé is not a job description. A job description details the tasks and responsibilities for a particular position; a résumé should identify an individual's strengths and accomplishments while performing such tasks.

When possible, a résumé should be tailored to specifically describe how an applicant meets the posted job requirements. It is a good idea to use the terms used in the job posting in the résumé. Often résumés may be scanned and analyzed by computer software that selects the résumés to be read by a recruiter.

Of course, many job applications are Internet-based, requiring job seekers to fill in blanks. I encourage job seekers to have critical job information, such as employment dates, skills, and personal references, summarized on a memo pad.

Do you think that résumés and cover letters are becoming less important because so many organizations are seeking applicants via their Internet sites?

# Christmas Day

What memories do you have of Christmas Day?

I grew up on a small farm near Hubbard, Texas, about seventy-five miles south of Dallas. My mother and her two sisters and their families always spent Christmas Day together. We opened our presents on Christmas Eve, and Christmas Day was filled with food, including turkey and dressing, candied yams, green beans, salad, and desserts of all types.

After lunch, the men frequently began to play "Forty-two," a game using twenty-eight dominoes. The women cleaned the kitchen and discussed the problems of the day or wondered about the actions of neighbors and friends. Then they would model their Christmas gifts. We children played with toys Santa had delivered and games such as hide-and-seek.

Have things changed? For my wife and me, spending time with our children and grandchildren is the highlight of the season. The food is still wonderful. Throughout the year, my wife buys special gifts for our grandchildren as we travel on cruises and car trips. These gifts are hidden in our home on Christmas Eve. Gifts for each grandchild are hidden in a designated room, and the search begins! The fun is watching the grandkids searching for their gifts. Even though the children are now much older—some are 21—they insist on this gift-searching tradition. Being with family and attending Christmas Eve church services are the memories that I will keep.

On reflection, I don't think that things have really changed that much. The day reminds me of family members who are no longer here that I miss—especially on this day. All in all, however, I think that today is even better than the "good old days"!

# Life's Routines and Finding Employment

Recently I have been thinking about how our lives are replete with daily and weekly routines. Do you have such routines that occupy your time?

For example, on every Wednesday my wife and I go to North Dallas Shared Ministries (NDSM), where we volunteer our time to assist people in need. Wednesday afternoon my wife attends a meeting of women in our condominium development. They discuss various current events and share a drop of wine and some nibbles during their discussions. Fridays are spent by my wife volunteering at NDSM and by me at SCORE. Saturday includes breakfast at Angela's. The Sunday schedule always includes church followed by lunch at the Corner Bakery, Fernando's, or Houston's. My Mondays frequently include the grading of papers from my Thursday night class. Tuesdays typically include lunch at the Black Eyed Pea.

As you can see, we are retired; however, I recall that days during my full-time work were also filled with routines. So I am thinking that job seekers may have also become trapped in a nest of routines. My concern here is that staying with unsuccessful routines that are not mentally challenging may result in not finding employment. I have heard many people say that continuing to do the same thing again and again and expecting different results is one definition of insanity.

So what is my message? I encourage all job seekers to review their weekly activities. Change something! There are numerous suggestions for job seekers contained in this book. I suggest that you make a weekly schedule that includes measurable job-seeking activities. Each Monday or perhaps Sunday night, you should review the results of the past week's accomplishments and plan activities for the coming week.

By developing a measurable work plan, I think you will greatly improve the possibility of becoming employed. Do you have routines that may inhibit your ability to become employed?

# New Year's Day

Do you consider New Year's Day a time to start anew, or do you consider New Year's Day simply a time to continue your existing path?

I suppose the answer to this question is that it depends. If you are pleased with your life and want it to continue with only some minor course corrections, then you should continue as you are. However, if the past year was not particularly kind to you, perhaps it is time to redefine your action program.

For individuals who are seeking employment or are unhappy with their present situation, New Year's Day can be an opportune time to change the strategy used in search of a satisfying employment and life.

Here are my suggestions for you to use in developing a new strategy:

- Objectives, or What – It is important that you clearly define your objectives for the new year. Objectives should meet the SMART test: specific, measurable, acceptable, reasonable, and time-based.

- Strategy or How – Based on your defined objectives, you should develop strategies in order to achieve your objectives.

Developing a strategy without first establishing clear objectives is the same as choosing a means of transportation for taking a trip before deciding where you are going. Here is an example that you might use as you develop your own strategy:

Objective defined:

- Specific – A position in retail – sales or operations

- Measurable – Hours per week in focused job search – twenty-five; contacts per week – five; interviews per week – two; job offers – three

- Acceptable – Criteria for yourself, family, and others, such as relocation, shift work, and travel required.

- Reasonable – What were your previous earnings salary range for the position you are seeking?

- Time-Based – Typically you can expect one month search time for each $10,000-per-year target salary.

Strategies: This book contains numerous ideas for identifying job opportunities and obtaining job offers, including résumé preparation, Internet searches, and interviewing skills. I continue to recommend extensive use of networking among friends and family, job fairs, nonprofit organizations, and previous work relationships as a proven strategy for locating and landing a job.

These steps may seem like too much work; however, give them a try and measure your results. Best wishes for a successful new year!

# A Time to Share!

As we enter December, we begin seeing opportunities to help the less fortunate. Many organizations have Christmas trees with the names of children as well as senior adults attached with messages containing individual wishes for Christmas. What is special about this season?

I personally begin thinking of family traditions and my father, mother, and brother, who are no longer with us. I have many memories of visits by Santa Claus and surprise presents.

This Christmas my wife and I will enjoy the company of our son, daughter, their spouses, and our five wonderful grandchildren. We are all in good health and have fulfilling lives. We are blessed.

I know for the unemployed this is a difficult time. Funds to purchase gifts may be limited, and feelings of self-pity may creep in. My suggestion is that you seek others who are less fortunate and be a friend to them with acts of kindness, such as serving meals and giving clothing. Everyone appreciates being told that his or her friendship is important.

# More Résumé Tips

A fellow job counselor of mine, Bob, at North Dallas Shared Ministries, www.ndsm.org, sent me the following tips about résumé writing provided at www.monster.com by Charles Purdy, Monster senior editor.

Your résumé needs an update—that is, if your résumé is like that of most people, it's not as good as it could be. The problem is language: Most résumés are a thicket of deadwood words and phrases—empty clichés, annoying jargon, and recycled buzzwords. Recruiters, HR folks, and hiring managers see these terms over and over again, and it makes them sad.

Wouldn't you rather make them happy? It's time to start pruning your résumé, starting with these (and similar) terms.

1. "Salary negotiable"

Yes, they know. If you're wasting a precious line of your résumé on this term, it looks as though you're padding—that you've run out of things to talk about. If your salary is not negotiable, that would be somewhat unusual. (Still, don't put that on your résumé either.)

2. "References available by request"

See the preceding comment about unnecessary terms.

## 3. "Responsible for _____"

Reading this term, the recruiter can almost picture the C-average, uninspired employee mechanically fulfilling his job requirements—no more, no less. Having been responsible for something isn't something you did—it's somethingthathappenedtoyou. Turn phrases like "responsible for" into "managed," "led," or other decisive, strong verbs.

## 4. "Experience working in _____"

Again, experience is something that happens to you— not something you achieve. Describe your background in terms of achievements.

## 5. "Problem-solving skills"

You know who else has problem-solving skills? Monkeys. Dogs. On your résumé, stick to skills that require a human.

## 6. "Detail-oriented"

So, you pay attention to details. Well, so does everyone else. Don't you have something unique to tell the hiring manager? Plus, putting this on your résumé will make that accidental typo in your cover letter or résumé all the more comical.

## 7. "Hardworking"

Have you ever heard the term "show—don't tell"? This is where that might apply. Anyone can call himself a hard worker. It's a lot more convincing if you describe situations in concrete detail in which your hard work benefited an employer.

## 8. "Team player"

See the preceding comment about showing instead of telling. There are very few jobs that don't involve working with someone else. If you have relevant success stories about collaboration, put them on your résumé. Talk about the kinds of teams you worked on, and how you succeeded.

## 9. "Proactive"

This is a completely deflated buzzword. Again, show rather than tell.

## 10. "Objective"

This term isn't always *verboten*, but you should use it carefully. If your objective is to get the job you've applied for, there's no need to spell that out on your résumé with its own heading.

A résumé objective is usually better replaced by a career summary describing your background, achievements, and what you have to offer an employer. An exception might be if you haven't applied for a specific job and don't have a lot of experience that speaks to the position you'd like to achieve.

# Cover Letters and Thank You Letters

An article on page 1J in *The Dallas Morning News* on October 23, 2011, "Cover Letters: Elements of Style," by Cliff Garinn, states that a cover letter gives an applicant another chance to emphasize what he or she can contribute to the target organization. Here are some of Garinn's tips:

- No spelling or typing errors.

- Address the letter to an individual who makes the hiring decision.

- Write the letter in a personal style.

- Refer to specifics about the organization and the open position.

- Indicate understanding of how you meet the job requirements and qualifications.

- Ask for a response by stating you are looking forward to a meeting.

I have found that a written response after an interview or any communication from the target organization is most important. Immediately after the meeting, you should send a thank you letter to the interviewer containing specific references to your conversation.

Perhaps an e-mail to the interviewer is sufficient. Anyway, I think that your communication should indicate your interest in the opportunity (assuming that you are interested) and that you look forward to the next meeting.

# Structure Your Résumé for the Situation

One résumé does not fit all situations! I am suggesting that you structure your résumé for the target audience. Almost everyone has accumulated many skills and experiences over his or her career.

As you review the requirements of the job you are seeking, you should revise your résumé to highlight specific areas of your background that meet the job requirements.

Another important point is to remember that a résumé is not a job description! The hiring organization has a clear understanding of the duties of the position it is seeking to fill. It is important that your résumé cite specific examples of your experience and accomplishments when you performed the advertised job requirements.

As many organizations use software systems to scan résumés for keywords, I suggest that you incorporate where possible appropriate words that the hiring organization included in its solicitation.

Included as appendix A to this book are résumés that I have used for business, academic, and volunteer environments.

# High-Energy Search or Go Fishing

I was speaking with a job counseling professional who expressed her concern about the lack of interest shown by job seekers. She and her husband provide weekly job counseling at a church in Dallas.

She said that recently very few individuals attend these free counseling sessions. She was puzzled about this poor showing by the unemployed.

I am hoping that this situation is not a trend but an isolated event. Nevertheless, I encourage all unemployed to take advantage of professionals who provide job search advice at no cost.

You should try an intense two-week regime filled with job search activities. If my advice yields no results, then go fishing!

# Merit Badges Replacing College Diplomas?

An article on page C3 in the *Wall Street Journal* on January 21, 2012, "Merit Badges for the Job Market," by Jeffrey R. Young, got my attention.

Young suggested that merit badges could replace college diplomas as evidence of a job seeker's competence. Young compares such experience badges with merit badges earned by Boy Scouts. The article states that many education reformers feel that the standard certification system no longer works in today's fast-changing market.

Such merit badges could be earned via the Internet. Peter Thiel, a founder of PayPal, offered selected students $100,000 not to go to college. He challenged each recipient to start a company instead of sitting in a lecture hall.

Young writes "Today, the Internet provides universal access to books and lectures and a fluid social network that lets any 19-year-old with an idea to find rich investors or flash a résumé to potential employers."

The article reminds me of Michael Dell and Bill Gates, who have done fairly well as college dropouts; however, it is interesting to note that Young, who wrote the article, has a law degree from Stanford University.

I am thinking that your résumé should include all badges that you have earned. Further, I do not think that having a college degree is a disadvantage to finding employment. Merit badges may be a great advantage and perhaps an organization's employment decision tiebreaker.

# SECTION III
# – NETWORKING

Almost every job counselor agrees that networking is probably the best strategy for finding jobs. A Google search will identify many articles that define how one should accomplish networking. An article by Meridith Levinson published in 2007, "How to Network: 12 Tips for Shy People" (www.cio.com/article/print/164300), is a fine example. I think that the word "proactive" describes the actions that a job seeker should take.

Finding a job is a full-time job! Job seekers should take advantage of all situations that may or may not yield a potential job opportunity. You never know which action or inaction may impact your life. Another important strategy to use in finding employment with networking is helping others, which is also a way to share your talents with the less fortunate. The good news is that as you are helping others improve their lives, you are also helping yourself find employment. What follows is information that addresses the important activity of networking.

# Reconnecting with Your Alma Mater

An article on page 1D in *The Dallas Morning News's* November 13, 2010, edition, "Alumni Seek Career Coaching," by Melissa Repko, provides examples of university career centers assisting graduates in finding employment.

While I personally have not used alumni counseling services provided by my schools, I think that universities are great resources for ex-students seeking employment.

In addition, I suggest job seekers reconnect with their favorite teachers. Many of these professors have contacts throughout industry.

# Job Searches and Social Networking

An article from McClatchy Newspapers on page A29 in the August 21, 2009, edition of *The Dallas Morning News*, titled "Before a Job Search, Put a Lid on Your Tweets," provided some very good advice about social networking.

Perhaps you can best define social networking by providing examples. How many social networks can you name? Let's see: Facebook, LinkedIn, Twitter, and MySpace are a few that come to mind.

"Every tweet, every post is being actively indexed by different search engines. It's going to be available in perpetuity," Gillian Gabriel, a headhunter for advertising and marketing agencies, was quoted as saying in the article.

I recall careers being marred when revealing pictures taken years ago became public. The advice here is that you should think twice or perhaps three times before you post negative thoughts or ideas on a social network.

Such words may be found by the organization with which you are seeking employment. I am wondering if negative thinking, speaking, or writing is ever beneficial to anything or anybody.

# Professional Career Help

Where can an unemployed person go to get some professional help finding employment? Several professional counseling organizations were mentioned in "Shop Around for the Right Career Professional," article by Cheri Butler on page 1J in the July 18, 2010 edition of *The Dallas Morning News.* Typically career counselors charge fees for their services.

Perhaps if you are unemployed, the last thing that you need is another expense. I suggest that you take advantage of church and civic organizations that offer free networking and counseling advice. The Texas Workforce Commission conducts job search seminars.

I volunteer at North Dallas Share Ministries in Dallas, which provides free job counseling Monday through Friday for its clients. Google, Yahoo, and Bing search engines identify many sites that provide free job counseling information.

# How to Network – Tips for Shy People

*CIO* magazine's December 11, 2007, edition had an article by Meridith Levinson (www.cio.com/article/print/164300) that provided the following tips for networking:

- Start small – Begin your networking efforts by seeking out familiar faces, such as relatives and friends.

- Stop apologizing – You do not have to apologize for asking for help or wanting to learn more about another person.

- Be yourself – Many introverted professionals think that they have to act like an extrovert. You do have to make an effort, but you should not appear artificial.

- Tap into your passion – You should join clubs and attend events that relate to your interest or activity, such as attending sporting events.

- Ask for introductions – You should be the first to introduce yourself to others.

- Be generous – You should share your ideas with others by contributing your experience in the conversation.

- Be prepared – You should have in mind several responses to typical questions, such as how is your job search going or how are you spending your day.

- Follow up – It is important that you follow through on what you have said to someone. For example, if you said you would provide a name and telephone number, you need to e-mail or call the person with the information.

- Get over your rejection – You will find people who do not want to help you or care about your situation. In such cases, move on down the road. As I say sometimes, "See a new round of cards."

- Take risks – You should be willing to make the first step to begin a conversation. You never know where a simple statement such as "How is your day going?" may lead.

- Seek a shrink – The article suggests if all else fails, you might see a therapist. My suggestion is that you find a mentor, close friend, or spouse to discuss your feelings and concerns. Sometimes when you verbalize your thinking, a plan of action will result.

# Fill Your Funnel!

I remember while attending sales school, the instructor asked the student salespersons to learn how to fill their funnels. As you know, a typical funnel is very large at the top and slopes to a small opening at its bottom.

The idea is that you identify as many sales suspects as possible, and you qualify the suspects, converting them to prospects. The objective is to focus on these prospects and hopefully close the orders. You certainly do not want to waste time and effort on suspects who cannot afford or have no need for your product or service.

I am thinking that job seekers should begin filling their funnels with job suspects early in a new year. Job seekers can qualify a job prospect by determining if an organization has open positions that meet their experience and skills.

With identified prospects, it is time to develop marketing strategies to win a job offer. We have previously discussed job-seeking marketing strategies, which include tailored résumés, cover letters, and follow-up techniques.

# Good Advice and Silver Bullets

The December 19, 2010, edition of *The Dallas Morning News* on page 1J contained an article by Amy Winter of Creators Syndicate about outplacement firm Challenger, Gray & Christmas's plans to provide free job advice to callers over a two-day period.

Some job advice tips include:

- Tell people about your job loss.

- Stay in touch with contacts.

- Do not put your job search on hold.

To me, there appears nothing new in these suggestions; however, the advice is good. I do not believe that there is a silver bullet you can use to find a job; hard work consisting of focusing on identifying opportunities and immediately taking action on such opportunities seems to me to be ammunition for your job search weapon.

# Executive Women Find Jobs!

An article on page 2D in *The Dallas Morning News* on October 24, 2010, by Cheryl Hall, "Executive Women Share Tips on Job Hunt," provided the following suggestions from four women who were out of work before finding executive positions:

To get a foot in the door:

- Get clear in your mind about what kind of position you want.

- Tell everyone you know exactly what you're looking for.

- Work your network as far back as possible.

- Target companies that fit your dream job.

- Stay busy. Do volunteer or contract work.

In the interview:

- Go in with a sense of culture. Visit the company website to see how people dress and how they "speak" in their bios and corporate information.

- Show how you'll plug in to the organization immediately.

- Be yourself. If they don't like you, it probably isn't a good fit.

- Be patient but persistent.

It is interesting to me that the advice from successful executive women is very similar to advice frequently given by recruiters and job counselors to all job seekers. Perhaps you should consider these suggestions as you seek employment.

# Be Ready to Go Social to Land A Job

An article in the November 29, 2009, issue of *The Dallas Morning News,* on page 1J, "Ready to Go Social to Land A Job," by ARAcontent, lists the following questions suggested by Marc Scoler, a career service professional to ask yourself as you prepare to network and socialize:

- What Industry is most interesting to you for a career? Why?

- What geographic location is most appearling?

- What duties do you enjoy doing most and least as they relate to your industry?

- What is the minimum pay you can survive on?

- What topics within your industry do you want to learn most about?

- What position do you want three to five years from now?

- What personal goals can you achieve by obtaining a position in your chosen industry?

- What is your ideal work schedule?

- What employer-offered benefits are important to you?

- What are some of the jobs titles that interest you?

- Whom can you contact within your industry of choice?

The questions by Marc Scoleri seem to describe the ideal position for a job seeker. Unfortunately, job seekers are not typically able to be so discriminating in this job market.

The article also quotes Victoria Snabon-Healt, a career executive, who says that socializing and networking are important and suggests the following ideas:

1. Joining and volunteering with professional organizations in your fields of interest.

2. Attending monthly meetings and social mixers.

3. Meeting hiring managers who are difficult to contact during business hours.

4. Putting yourself out there; it's who you know that can help get you in the door, and it's what you know that keeps you there.

# Networking and Associations

On July 10, 2010, I participated in the graduation exercises for the University of Phoenix's (UOP) Dallas Campus at Cowboys Stadium in Arlington, Texas.

In attendance were about 1,400 graduates, 75 faculty, and 4,000 friends and family. The keynote speaker, Dr. Jeff Kaplan of the Greenlight Research Group, discussed the importance of networking for the graduates.

He indicated that there were a million or more UOP graduates and that this group is a great source of career opportunities for all UOP graduates.

Based on Kaplan's remarks, I am thinking that all job seekers have associations with friends, family, and previous coworkers who can provide assistance in finding employment and business opportunities.

I suggest that you make a list of possible contacts from your previous life who may provide you job leads and business opportunities. In addition, this group may also become your personal references, which employers will request of all job applicants.

The time you spend in networking will pay dividends!

# Networking and Religious Organizations

As I have frequently written, I believe that networking is a key strategy in finding a job. I want to encourage all job seekers to pursue becoming involved in social organizations—particularly with religious organizations.

Why religious organizations? I believe that religious organizations by their very nature are caring and interested in the welfare of their members and associates. Many such organizations have activities for individuals seeking employment.

You may want to check out these websites, which contain employment leads:

http://www.christianet.com/christianjobs/ - ChristianNet – The Worldwide Christian Commmunity

http://www.rileyguide.com/support.html - The Riley Guide: Network, Interview, & Negotiate or Handling a Job Loss

http://www.supportworks.org/cat756.htm-SupportWorks Online

# Making a List!

The December 18, 2011, edition of *The Dallas Morning News* had two articles on page 1J that dealt with the issue of stopping job searches: "Don't Stop Looking during the Holidays," by Cheri Butler, and "Pros and Cons of Putting Off Job Search," by Lindsay Novak of Creators Syndicate.

Both articles encourage job seekers not to delay their searches by taking time off for the holiday season or a sabbatical after completing school or leaving a job.

I am not Santa, but I suggest that job seekers make a list of things they could do during the Christmas and holiday seasons:

1. During family gatherings, discuss your situation with relatives. You may be surprised at the possible contacts you may discover.

2. When attending social gatherings, work the room, introduce yourself around, and start conversations concerning work-related subjects.

3. At your church or volunteer organizations, determine if they have job counseling or networking meetings.

4. While visiting shopping malls, check to see postings for open positions.

Of course, you should spend time each day with our friend the Internet. In my blog, I post many sites for job seekers.

If only one of these ideas encourages you to continue your job search, I will be pleased.

# Summer Heat and Job Search!

As we begin to endure many days of one hundred-plus–degree weather, I am tempted to stay in the house and enjoy air-conditioning! However, I am fortunate enough to be a retired person with a comfortable income.

As an active retired person, I spent fourteen hours the previous day as an election clerk. I will be attending a luncheon as I write this for the SCORE organization for which I am the chapter chair.

This week I am completing grading and posting grades for a graduate MBA course at the University of Phoenix's Dallas Campus. Later in the week, I will serve as an interviewer at the North Dallas Shared Ministries in Dallas.

So you say, so what! I am suggesting that job searchers schedule their week with activities focused on finding a job. Staying at home and avoiding the heat may improve your attitude, but it will not assist you in becoming employed.

# Finding the Hiring Organization

I periodically serve as a job counselor at North Dallas Shared Ministries (www.ndsm.org). Many of my clients seeking employment do not own computers, and some have no computer skills. As I try to assist them, I find many job postings on sites such as Monster.com, Craiglist.com, hotJobs.com, and Indeed.com. Unfortunately, job seekers are required to post their résumés online, and the hiring company is frequently not disclosed.

Finding the hiring organization requires some detective work on my part. Based on the information provided in the ad, I am often able to navigate to the hiring company's website, where I can find telephone numbers and addresses. It is up to the job seeker to contact the hiring company and request an interview.

Clients who post their résumés on job boards many times never receive responses. Rather than waiting for a reply that may or may not occur, I suggest a proactive approach.

An article on page 1J in the May 15, 2011, issue of Tthe *Dallas Morning News*, "Internet Isn't the Only Way to Finding a Job," by Amy Winter of Creators Syndicate, quoted John A. Challenger, CEO of Challenger, Gray & Christmas, who suggested visiting company websites to obtain valuable contact information. The job seeker should e-mail the hiring person and include specifics about his or her qualifications and experience. Further, I think it is important for the job seeker to state that he or she is immediately available and ready to get to work!

For job seekers without an Internet connection or a computer, I suggest visiting the local library. Typically public libraries have computers connected to the Internet available for their members.

# More Job Openings
# Than Qualified Candidates!

I attended the 5th Annual Technology Trends Conference at the Hilton Dallas Lincoln Centre Hotel on October 7, 2011. Many knowledgeable executives, educators, and professionals discussed what the future might hold for new developments in technology.

One speaker stated that there was no shortage of jobs, but there was a shortage of qualified candidates. I thought about this statement and wondered if it was actually true. As a job counselor at the North Dallas Shared Ministries, I visit with many unemployed people who have been unsuccessful in finding jobs. Where are these job openings, I wonder?

I have spent much of my business career with organizations that focused on increasing the productivity of workers by automating routine tasks such as answering telephones, posting payments to accounts, and storing and retrieving business records. Many of the remaining or restructured jobs required specialized skills and/or critical thinking. So what is the takeaway message to job seekers?

I encourage job seekers to take maximum advantage of their experience and knowledge. If there are no jobs in their field of expertise, they need to find areas to which their experience can be transferred. Many departing military personnel face this situation. Another point is that if you have no specialty, you should seek the training to build one. For example, many jobs are available for driving commercial vehicles. Why not attend training and secure a commercial driver's license? As an information systems person, I suggest that you become proficient in commonly used software products, including the Internet.

# Blue-Collar Workers in Short Supply

An article on page 6P in *The Dallas Morning News's* January 22, 2012, edition, "In Short Supply: Blue-Collar Workers," by Joel Kotkin, discussed the need for skilled workers.

Kotkin quoted Karen Wright, CEO of Ariel Corp of Mount Vernon, Ohio, as saying, "My biggest problem isn't the lack of work; it's a lack of skilled workers. We have a very skilled workforce, but they are getting older."

The article was very persuasive about the lack of skilled workers in the United States.

Kotkin wrote, "The oversupply of college-educated workers is especially striking when you contrast it with the growing shortage of skilled manufacturing workers."

What is the message for job seekers? As you search for jobs, you should consider skilled positions. If organizations are in need of such workers, perhaps training positions are available.

I think that the term *blue collar* has a demeaning connotation in that it implies only manual labor. The term *skilled worker* invokes a very different image and should be used by organizations seeking employees.

If you are unemployed with a college degree, I suggest that you should consider skilled-worker positions.

# Feminine Traits Can Strengthen Business

An article on page 1J in *The Dallas Morning News's* November 14, 2010, edition, "Tips for Seasonal Workers," by Amy Winters of Creators Syndicate, discussed how seasonal positions can become full-time jobs.

However, I think that the most interesting part of the article discussed how feminine traits can help companies thrive as social media change.

Quoting Barry Libert, author of *Social Nation: How to Harness the Power of Social Media to Attract Customers, Motivate Employees, and Grow Your Business,* the article discussed how the following feminine traits, when exhibited by both women and men, can result in improved leadership:

- Get to know your workers. Understand what motivates them and what encourages them to come to work every day.

- Ask for help. If you aren't sure how to do something, don't be afraid to ask for other opinions. It is OK to collaborate, even when you are the leader.

- Let others lead sometime. Pass the power down and allow others to be in charge when needed.

- Listen to your leadership group.

- Try to gain better self-awareness. Attempt to understand how your workers view you. Are you intimidating? Are you unapproachable and not willing to help?

- Be open to a social culture. This type of culture will allow employee talent to develop and grow, leading to a positive impact for the company.

- Focus on others. It isn't all about you. It is about team building and developing a faithful and positive workforce.

# SECTION IV – EMPLOYMENT WEBSITES AND JOB FAIRS

The Internet has become a major resource for both job seekers and employers. However, individuals must be careful when posting personal information in response to job ads. Websites come and go, so many of the sites listed in this section may have been changed or removed. Many job postings do not include specific contact information for the actual employing organization. However, some detective work may disclose the name of the organization.

# A Link to Finding Public Service Jobs

Certainly a fast-growing segment of our economy is government services. This website may be helpful as you seek employment:

USAJOBS – Working for America - http://www.usajobs.gov/

This website provides links to federal, state, local, and even tribal job sites.

I recommend that all job seekers review the job postings available on this site.

# Avoid Job-Hunt Scams

An article in the October 9, 2009, edition of *USA Today* by Walecia Konrad cautions job seekers to be aware of the following possible scams:

- Stimulus come-ons. Any e-mail from a government agency listing job openings based on the federal stimulus plan is bogus. The government is recruiting, but not by this type of e-mail.

- Bogus interview invites. Any e-mail inviting you to go to a distant city for an interview and encouraging you to use a discounted travel agency to purchase tickets probably is a ploy to get your credit card information.

- Bad guys on good sites. Do not respond to job sites with personal information such as your address and Social Security number. It is better to ask the potential employer to contact you by telephone or for a face-to-face interview.

Personal information is sacred and should be carefully guarded.

# Searching the Internet for Jobs

I am a volunteer job counselor at North Dallas Shared Ministries. While I have a number of favorite links for job searches, I frequently use the following strategy:

1. On the Internet, go to google.com.

2. Enter on the search line: "jobs city keyword1 keyword2 keyword3." An example: "jobs Dallas accounting budgeting payroll."

3. The search typically finds a number of sites containing employment opportunities.

This method is not always fruitful; however, it is always a good starting point. I suggest that you try this strategy to see if it works for you.

# Social Networking and Job Searches

I found the following website that rates the effectiveness of ten top social nNetworking sites:

2012 Social Networking Websites Comparisons -

http://social-networking-websites-review.toptenreviews. com/

As job seekers develop strategies to aid in finding jobs, social networking may be a beneficial approach. Networking is an effective way to contact individuals who may in turn introduce a job seeker to potential employers.

# LinkedIn.com – Potential Valuable Networking Site

An article in the November 8, 2009, issue of *The Dallas Morning News,* "Know How to Use Online Job-Search Tools," by Cheri Butler, asked whether the Internet is a crutch or a valuable tool. She says that LinkedIn.com has become a most respected site for social networking and job searches.

Butler stressed the importance of just plain networking. Finding a job is a full-time job. Just waiting for the telephone to ring or for an e-mail containing a job offer to arrive may prove disappointing. I suggest that you become a proactive person and make every day a workday—searching for a job.

# "Don't Neglect the Classifieds When Job Hunting"

An article in the December 27, 2009, issue of *The Dallas Morning News,* "Don't Neglect the Classifieds When Job Hunting," quotes Cheri Butler, associate director of career services at the University of Texas Arlington, as saying:

"Some employers won't post job openings on the major online job sites. Maybe they want to avoid being overwhelmed with applicants, or maybe they just want to find the best local candidates without attracting job seekers from throughout the country. The fact is, if you're not scanning the newspaper classified, you're missing out on an opportunity."

Perhaps this article is a bit self-servicing for the newspaper; however, I think if you are a job seeker, it is worth your time to review job postings in local newspapers.

# Happy New Year 2010!

Here is a December 2009 letter written to Crabby, Curt MacRae. *Curt MacRae is Michigan father who was forced to shut down his 15-year-old business and file for bankruptcy. While looking for work he runs workshops that help other unemployed people jump-start their careers.* I think that the resolutions may be helpful to unemployed job seekers:

*Dear Crabby,*

*I wrote some resolutions for the New Year. 2009 was not my finest year, and I am thinking that I need to do something about it in 2010. My job search seemed to stall. There were some things I wanted to change anyway, and maybe those will help my search.*

*It's time to be proactive, positive, and productive, and to that end, I wanted to share these resolutions and ask if you had any to add. Thanks for being there this year; I hope you'll stay with us in 2010.*

*Proactive in Pittsburgh*

*2010 Resolutions*

- I resolve to lose forty pounds. While that shouldn't make a difference in my job search, perhaps this added weight is affecting people's opinions as to whether I can do my job, or if I have enough drive to accomplish a goal; I'm going to drive to accomplish that goal now.

- I am going to appreciate my family, my friends, my community, and I'm going to let them know it. Sometimes it's easy, when times are tough, to ignore those relationships that are strongest and most important. I want to keep those strong.

- I'm going to take time for me; I'm going to learn something new, or play an instrument, or get involved in a sports league or volunteer work that makes me feel good.

- I will dedicate one day each week to the job boards. I will reset my search criteria and get e-mails only once per week; will that hinder my search? Companies are moving so slowly in hiring anyway, it seems to make sense, and it will reduce my stress levels. I'm wasting time looking at every e-mail as it comes into my mailbox.

- I will attend at least one networking event each week, and I will focus not only on events for those out of work but also business events where I can mingle with working people.

- I will target companies I want to work for, and I will research those companies so I'll be well-informed when I talk to hiring managers.

- I plan to stay positive: It is easy to get down, and I have from time to time, especially when all of the interviews have not panned out the way I had hoped. Rejection is part of this game, so the more work I do, the more rejections I may get, but that simply means the closer I will be to landing a new position.

- I'll invest some of my time into a good, ongoing support group/workshop with other people who are looking for new opportunities. It's a good time to network, share in positive reinforcement, and gain some new insights and ideas for my job search (one good idea that nets me a shot can make my time investment a huge money saver).

- I will write down my goals, both personal and professional, by January 1, 2010, and I will monitor those all year.

Crabby, that's about it, and obviously some other tasks will tag along with these nine. I wanted to share these with your readers and see if you, or any of your readers, would like to suggest more.

# New Internet Websites
# Coming for Job Searches!

An article on page 1J in the March 3, 2010, edition of *The Dallas Morning News*, "Refreshing the Online Job Search," by Christopher Rugaber, discussed how Bill Warren, founder of Monster.com, was starting a non-profit job listing system.

The organization, named DirectEmployers Association, was formed by 500 large companies. According to the article, "The association's plans call for companies to list jobs under the Internet's .job domain name. For example, someone can visit ATT.jobs to see all the job listings by AT&T."

The posting cost through the DirectEmployers Association will be much less than that charged by commercial job boards such as Monster.com. This new job site is an exciting development for all job seekers and employers!

# Internet Job Sites for Veterans

Searches of Google, Yahoo, Bing, and other search engines turn up a number of Internet sites that post job opportunities for veterans.

I encourage all veterans to go to these sites in search of jobs.

I send my respect, admiration, and appreciation for all who serve and have served our country.

# Overseas Jobs for Americans

An article by Norimitsu Onishi of *The New York Times* that ran on page 33A in the September 19, 2010, edition of the *Dallas Morning News* discussed OFWs—"overseas Filipinos workers"—and got me thinking about possible jobs for Americans overseas.

I did a Google search on "overseas jobs for Americans" and was frankly surprised at the number of postings. For example, you might check out these websites:

U.S. Government Jobs in Europe

http://www.jobmonkey.com/europejobs/us-government-jobs.html,

Jobs with American and Overseas Contractors in the Gulf States, Yemen and other overseas Countries in the Region - http://www.jobline.net/jobiraq1.htm,

Jobs Abroad Search - http://www.jobsabroad.com,

AnAmericanAbroad.com International Jobs for Americans - http://www.anamericanabroad.com/jobs.html

Overseas work may require sacrifices and hardships; however, the compensation may be sufficient for you to pursue the opportunities.

# Social Networking and Finding a Job

Many articles and postings discuss the use of social networking by job seekers and employers. Major social networks include Facebook, MySpace, Twitter, and LinkedIn. Here are some Internet postings that provide opinions concerning the use of these networks.

"Social Networking Can Be Perilous to Your Employment." Recruiters search postings on the Internet so you should not post any personal information that might be detrimental to your job search. Please refer to Yahoo Voices using the following link: http://www.associatedcontent.com/article/61351/social_networking_can_be_perilous_to.html?cat=31

An article posted on September 19, 2008, by Daniel Schwartz, professor at Stanford University, New York City states:

"Overall, employers should tread very carefully in using social networking sites as a screening device. There are very little substantive advantages to using such sites, and there are several landmines employers need to avoid. While they may satisfy an employer's curiosity, the time-worn principles of checking references, conducting interviews and, if necessary, background screening, should typically satisfy most employers' need to hire the best candidate."

Using Social Networking Sites for Employment Screening: Is there a Right Answer?

"Do's and Don'ts of Social Networking When Looking for Work," an article by Metro Editorial published September 28, 2010, contains a list of suggestions for job seekers to follow. This article is available at the following Sentinel Source.com link:

http://sentinelsource.com/articles/2010/09/28/business/news/free/doc4ca212f93b324939269200.txt

My advice to job seekers is to post nothing on a social network that they would not say in a fully loaded elevator moving to the top of an office building or in any public space. One never knows who may be listening. Many individuals enjoy being a source for the "grapevine.""

# Internet Job Search Sites

*The Dallas Morning News,* on page 1J of its February 20, 2011, edition, had an article by Amy Winter of Creators Syndicate that suggested that job seekers should look beyond their local area for jobs. Listed in the article were the following job sites:

www.dice.com – technical jobs

www.computer.com – technical jobs

www.journalismjobs.com – journalism jobs

www.creativehotlist.com – visual communication jobs

www.burryman.com – freelance writing jobs

www.idealist.org – nonprofit jobs

www.idealist.org – nonprofit jobs

www.lawjobs.com – law jobs

www.ratracerbellion.com – work-at-home jobs (Creators Syndicate site)

www.workplacelikehome.com – work-at-home jobs

www.monster.com – general categories

www.careerbuilder.com – general categories

<u>www.indeed.com</u> – general categories

I recognize there must be a thousand job sites; how-ever, this list is at least a starting point. Here are a few suggestions provided by the article:

- In the title of the position you are requesting, enter the title and a plus sign and/or the word *telecom-mute* or *telecommuting*.

- Do not enter your zip code, state, and other infor-mation that might place a limitation on you.

- Other possible words to include in your applica-tion are independent contractor, work from home, offsite, virtual, remote, freelance, and anywhere.

# The Dallas Morning News and Monster!

While reviewing *The Dallas Morning News's* February 13, 2011, edition, in the Jobs section on page 1J, I noticed there were many job postings with a job number and a Monster logo at the bottom of each posting. Job seekers should check out this new approach to finding jobs.

Many employers are now using media other that print to advertise their job openings. Years ago the News' jobs listings filled over several pages; now the job listings are less than one page.

# Job Fairs Again

*The Dallas Morning News* in an article on page 1J of its January 31, 2010, issue, "How to Get the Most from a Job Fair," by Cheri Butler, listed tips to job seekers attending job fairs. While other passages in this book indicate that job fairs are a waste of time, I think that if you are looking for a job, all avenues are open.

Here are some of the tips:

- Dress for the occasion.

- Identify companies you want to contact before going to the fair.

- Prepare a thirty-second personal introduction.

- Using a map of the fair, develop a plan to maximize your time.

- Get business cards at each booth for subsequent follow-up.

- Move through the fair alone and not with your buddies.

- Carry a nice portfolio and not a briefcase.

# Jobs for Military Personnel Seeking Civilian Employment Opportunities

An article in *USAA Magazine's* fall 2011 edition on page 13, "On the Job Front," by Greg Campbell, provided a great deal of advice for military personnel who are seeking civilian jobs. I am sure that you can obtain a copy of this magazine by contacting the United Services Automobile Association at 800-235-1898.

Here is a list of selected websites that have employment opportunities:

- Amazon – Online retailer: *www.amazon.com/b?ie=UTF8&node=2895924011*

- BNSF Railway – Railway: www.bnsf.com/careers/military

- Capstone - Defense contractor: www.capstone-corp.com

- Chesapeake Energy – Energy: www.chk.com/Careers

- Cintas – Corporate apparel: www.cintas.com/hr/military.asp

- Concurrent Technologies – R&D: www.ctc.com

- CSX Transportation – Railroads: www.csx.com

- DaVita – Health care: www.careers.davita.com

- Dollar General – Retail: www.dollargeneral.com/careers

- Fluor – Engineering and construction: www.fluor.com/military

- General Electric – Diversified financials: www.ge.com/military

- ManTech International – National security: www.mantech.com/careers

- Northrop Grumman – Aerospace/defense: www.careers.northropgrumman.com

- Schlumberger – Oil field services: www.careers.slb.com

- Schneider National – Trucking: www.schneider-jobs.com

- Sears Holding Corp. – Retail: www.searsholdings.com/careers

- Sprint – Telecommunications: http://careers.sprint.com

- Transocean – Offshore drilling: www.deepwater.com/fw/main/career-222.html

- URS, Federal Services – Engineering and construction: www.urscorp.com/careers

- USAA – Financial services: www.usaa.apply2jobs.com/profext/careers.html

- Verizon Communication – Telecommunications: http://www22.verizon.com/jobs

- Waste Management – Waste: www.wm.com/careers/index.jsp

Even if you are not a job seeker returning from the military, these sites are a good resource for locating employment opportunities.

# Internet Job Search Engines

Below is an updated list of Internet job search engines. More information about these sites is available from the article accessible through this address:

http://www.pcmag.com/article2/0,2817,2342783,00. asp#fbid=R0kuJ7iUl8e.

http://www.beyond.com/

Beyond.com claims to be the "largest network of niche career communities" on the Net. It essentially hooks together different organizations such as PRJobForce. com and PhillyJobs.com all in one place, which makes it easy to find leads in your community.

http://www.careerbuilder.com/

As the web's biggest job site, CareerBuilder gets more than twenty-three million visitors a month. The company has been around since 1995, and it has developed an incredible network of listing sources and job search centers since that time.

http://www.craigslist.org/

The granddaddy of online classifieds gives those who are focused on searching for jobs within their communities an easy way to look. It might be one of the least-polished entities listed here, but the sheer number of local job listings makes up for it.

http://www.hound.com/

Hound's search engine shows jobs from employer websites only. In theory, this cuts out duplicate listings and shows opportunities that are not posted on other job boards.

http://www.indeed.com/

Indeed works as an aggregator for listings from major job websites, company websites, associations, and other online sources. Its simplicity and ease of use are its best features.

http://www.jobcentral.com/

JobCentral is a service formed by a nonprofit consortium of U.S. corporations such as IBM and Dell, which makes it ideal if you're looking for corporate job listings.

http://www.jobserve.us/

JobServe claims it was "the world's first Internet recruitment service." In 2008, JobServe advertised more than 2.5 million jobs across fifteen industry sectors.

http://www.linkedin.com/

Best known for being a social network for professionals, LinkedIn also has thorough job listings, some of which are exclusive to LinkedIn.

http://www.monster.com/

In addition to being arguably the best-known global job-listings site, Monster also offers advice on résumés, interviewing, and salary information.

http://www.oodle.com/job/

Oodle, which specializes in online classifieds, includes a job classifieds section that finely cuts job opportunities down to job title, category, industry, and company. Did you know, for example, that Best Buy has nearly 10,000 openings as of publication?

http://www.ontargetjobs.com/

OnTargetJobs owns a lot of smaller niche sites such as BioSpace.com and MedHunters.com. Its expansive niche database allows users to find compatible job listings more easily than with general sites.

http://www.simplyhired.com/

SimplyHired is similar to Indeed, as it also aggregates listings from major job websites, newspapers, company websites, and associations. However, the site goes a little deeper and allows users to send their résumés out for posting on five other sites for free.

http://www.snagajob.com/

SnagAJob is basically the antithesis of sites like TheLadders and Execu|Search, as its focus is on hourly employment only. The site has partnered with companies such as 7-Eleven, Red Lobster, and AMF to bring the most up-to-date hourly job openings.

http://www.theladder.com

This job site has branded itself as the place to look for $100,000+ jobs only. Job seekers have to pay $30 per month to fully take advantage of the site's services.

http://www.trovix.com/

Trovix's free search engine makes the job-search process more personalized. Users input their work experience and qualifications, and the site matches results to what info they have given. Trovix also has an innovative feature called Job Map, which allows you to type in your location and see on Google Maps how many jobs are available in your area.

http://www.tweetmyjobs.com/

One of the newest sites to take advantage of social media, TweetMyJobs supplies Twitter users with instantaneous job listings that are derived from TweetMyJobs' Job Channels.

http://www.usajobs.com/

USAJobs is the official job site for the U.S. government. With the government looking to significantly increase spending during the next few years, looking at federal jobs might not be a bad move if you're in a tough place.

http://hotjobsonline.net

As one of the biggest job sites on the web, HotJobs distinguishes itself by focusing on features such as status (which shows how many times one's résumé has been viewed) and the ability to block companies from seeing your résumé.

# Worldwide Websites

I received a complimentary e-mail about my blog from Serg, an employee of the Jooble Company. Jooble.com is a website that provides job listings for the United States and many other countries.

More information about Jooble is available by contacting: Ladoburn Holdings LTDKimonos, 43AP.C. 3095, Limassol, Cyprus.

Listings of U.S.-based jobs can be found at www.jooble-us.com.

# Try the Employment Guide Website!

Every time I search the Internet for sites to assist job seekers in finding jobs, I find even more sites.

I suggest checking out EmploymentGuide.com, a site that provides the facility to search by job type and location.

# 9/11 Job Opportunities!

Where were you on September 11, 2001? I was completing my workout at the Cooper Aerobatic Center in Dallas. I remember being drawn to the TV in the locker room, which displayed pictures of New York City and the World Trade Center. At that moment I had no idea about the significance of this event.

I was wondering what new jobs have been created as a result from the 9/11 events. As you would expect, many of the new jobs are related to public security and our protection, including police forces and the U.S. military services. In addition, new products are now in the market, including alarms and security devices.

To locate more jobs and product opportunities, I suggest you use the following search arguments on Google, Bing, Yahoo, or other search engines: "911 jobs," "911hotjobs," "911 products," and the like.

# Internet Links to Home-Based Jobs

An article on page 1J in T*he Dallas Morning News's* October 9, 2011, edition, "Five Home-Based Jobs with a Social Side," by Christine Durst and Michael Haaren of Creators Syndicate, mentioned the following websites that provide listings for home-based jobs:

- www.Narms.com

I think the website of the National Association for Retail Marketing Services is very rich, with many additional links to jobs and information related to home-based businesses.

- http://assemblersinc.net

Assemblers Inc. is a leading provider of merchandise assembly, installation, delivery, and repair services that operates throughout the southeast United States.

- www.taskrabbit.com

This site has coverage of only a few cities; however, it provides leads for errand runners and other task handlers and may provide ideas to job seekers.

# SECTION V –
# INTERVIEW
# TECHNIQUES

Even though many jobs are listed on the Internet, in almost all cases, the job applicant and the personnel of the hiring organization meet face-to-face in order to evaluate each other and determine if there is a match. What follows are postings from my blog that provide insight and hopefully valuable suggestions for job seekers.

# How to Ace an Interview

The *Parade* magazine insert in the September 6, 2009, issue of *The Dallas Morning News* had advice for a job interview in an article titled "You Can Get a Job Now!" by Brad Dunn. The following are suggestions given in the "How to Ace an Interview" section:

- Prepare, prepare, prepare. Know about the company you are interviewing and be able to discuss three examples of your accomplishments that illustrate your abilities to fill the job.

- Keep answers short. The average American listens for twenty-eight seconds before becoming distracted.

- When in doubt, overdress. You never lose points by wearing formal business attire.

- Be positive. Never say anything negative about anyone or any organization.

- Ask for the job. Declare your interest in the job.

- Follow up promptly. Within one or two business days, send a brief thank you note to the interviewer. Add any comment that you feel that you should have made during the interview.

# Truth in Interviews and Confessionals

An important point to remember in an interview is to respond truthfully to questions asked by the interviewer. As an interviewer at North Dallas Shared Ministries, I ask clients many questions about their situations.

Frequently, clients respond to my questions with answers they think I want to hear. In a recent case, I asked a client if she was working at the restaurant listed on her interview sheet. She said yes, but her work hours had been reduced so assistance was needed. One telephone call to the employer resulted in my learning that the client had failed to report to work as scheduled and was fired. The restaurant said the client was not eligible for rehire.

In another interview, the client assured me that the address listed as place of residence was correct. A call to the apartment manager discovered that the client had moved two weeks prior. Such responses to an interviewer's questions can damage an applicant's credibility. Please assume that all information provided in an interview or on a résumé will be verified before a hiring decision is made.

On the other hand, an interview is not a confessional session. I suggest that you refrain from making any negative comments about yourself, any person, or any organization.

# Dress for Success Tips for Job Interviews

An article in the November 8, 2009, issue of *The Dallas Morning News,* on page 1J, "You've Gotten the Interview—Now Dress for Success," by North American Precis Syndicate, suggested the following tips as you dress for a job interview:

- Consider the industry: Every industry has its own set of style rules. For example, workers at banks and accounting and law firms tend to wear business suits, while those in creative industries such as advertising agencies and marketing firms often wear business casual.

- Do your homework: You can research the organization and its employees by driving by the company and observing the employees arrive and depart, or you might go online to view photos of company personnel. Take your cue from how the employees dress.

- Be polished: You need to make sure your clothing and appearance is in good order: no wrinkles, shoes shined, and hair kept. I personally do not care for visible tattoos and piercings.

- Leave any luxury or designer clothing and accessories at home: High-end handbags and watches that cost thousands of dollars may make you look frivolous.

- Make a favorable impression: "Wear one thing that reflects your personality and creativity," says Amy Goodman, a columnist. "A colorful tie, heirloom earrings, shoes with a unique design, or an eye-catching watch may be what helps an interviewer remember you from a sea of candidates."

# Rallying from Rejection

How does one deal with rejection by a potential employer? An article on page 1J in the December 13, 2009, edition of *The Dallas Morning News,* by Ralph Lee of MultiAd Builder, "Rallying from Rejection", suggests the following ideas for dealing with job rejection:

- Sometimes, the other applicant is just a better fit for the job.

- Don't take rejection personally.

- Don't let it negatively impact other parts of your life.

- Be prepared for rejection.

- Rejection could be a blessing in disguise.

- Handle the rejection tactfully.

- Just one "yes" is all you need.

From personal experience, I agree with the above ideas. I know that a positive attitude is the key to success in all endeavors, including finding a job. Further, energy is also important from both an internal and external perspective.

# I Cannot Believe This Has Happened to Me

A friend of mine gave me a copy of the January 2010 issue of the magazine *Think – Current Issues from a Distinctly Christian View.* She suggested that I read the article "I Cannot Believe This Has Happened to Me" on pages 28–29.

Here are some interesting facts and ideas contained in the article:

- Since 2007 the U.S. unemployed have increased from 7.6 million to 15.1 million.

- How do you eat an elephant? One bite at a time.

- The loss of a job is one of the most emotionally trying times a person can endure. Emotions such as confusion, betrayal, resentment, anxiety, and fear are quite common in the first few days.

- The following are logical steps for developing a job search plan:

- Make a list of people (at least twenty-five to fifty) you know who may have access to job opportunities. Make contact with them either in person or by telephone, text, or e-mail. Studies show that 80 percent–85 percent of positions are filled through referrals and not by applying to advertised jobs.

- Revise your résumé. Highlight your strengths, quantify your results, and be professional in your presentation.

- Practice answering questions about yourself and your strengths and weaknesses.

- Develop what many professionals call your "elevator speech"—a 30-second summary describing who you are and what benefits you can provide to a prospective employer.

- Be careful about developing a résumé and posting it on any and every job board. Be selective and protective when it comes to distributing your personal information.

- Execute your job plan during business hours. Reaching out to your network during the day presents a more professional image. Use the evening to summarize your progress and plan the next day.

- Follow up, both on résumés that you have submitted and with members of your network. Be professional without being a nuisance.

- After your interview, follow up with that person through a handwritten card or note. This is a nice touch and leaves a lasting impression.

- Jobs will not fall out of the sky. Maintain a positive attitude and professional approach in your search.

- Look toward the future. Plan for improving your position in the job world, but on the other hand, prepare yourself that you may be forced into taking a position that is less than anticipated.

- Believe in yourself and guidance from above.

# Where There Is Smoke

*The Dallas Morning News* in an article on page 1J in its January 24, 2010, issue, "Don't Let Your Looks Blow Your Interview," by NewsUSA, provided some suggestions for proper interview dress.

However, I am thinking that proper hygiene is also very important. One should give attention to his or her fingernails, facial hair, piercings, and hair.

Another consideration is your breath. I think that the scent of smoke on one's breath or clothes is an indication of a smoking habit. HR managers may be alert to signs of future health problems and related insurance premiums.

# Improve Your Interviewing Skills

*The Dallas Morning News* in an article on page 1J in its April 4, 2010, issue, "Job Seekers Should Improve Interview Skills," by Amy Winter of Creators Syndicate, listed the following examples of poor interviewing skills:

- Candidate wore a business suit with flip-flops.

- Candidate asked if the interviewer wanted to meet for a drink after the interview.

- Candidate had applied for an accounting job, yet said he was bad at managing money.

- Candidate ate food in the employee break room after the interview.

- Candidate recited poetry.

- Candidate applying for a customer services job said, "I don't really like working with people."

- Candidate had to go immediately to get his dog that had gotten loose in the parking lot.

- Candidate looked at the ceiling during the interview.

- Candidate used Dungeons and Dragons as an example of teamwork.

- Candidate filed fingernails.

I am sure that no readers of this book have used any of the above actions during a job interview.

# Maintain Qualified Work and Personal References

I provided job counseling one day to several out-of-work individuals. Two of my clients had lost their jobs because of absence from work or inability to adequately perform their jobs.

I asked them if they had a reference from their previous employer. They said that they had lost contact with employees whom they knew. One client said that the employees she knew had left the organization and she had no contact information. One client told me that her only reference was her husband.

My advice to them was that they should attempt to contact someone who could provide a credible reference. I believe that almost all hiring organizations will ask applicants for a reference from a previous employer.

My suggestion to all readers is that they negotiate business and personal references. One never knows when the unemployment event may occur.

# Watch Out for Scams!

An article on page 19A in *The Dallas Morning News's* November 6, 2010, edition, "Scams Target the Jobless," by Stuart Pfeifer of the *Los Angeles Times,* discussed how a weak job market makes job seekers vulnerable to scammers who seek to bilk them out of their money.

Here are some suggestions as to how to avoid job scams:

- Beware of employers who ask for money up front for training and materials.

- Be cautious of placement services that guarantee they'll find you a job.

- Check out companies with the Better Business Bureau or through a Google search.

- Do not cash unsolicited checks that arrive in the mail. Endorsing and cashing such instruments may obligate you contractually to terms and conditions for which you are unaware.

- Be careful with placement agencies that direct you to call a toll-free number. Sometimes these companies can transfer you, without your knowledge, to a number that charges a fee.

- Follow up with the corporate offices listed in the ad by an employment service to find if that firm really is hiring.

- Do not give your credit card or bank information over the telephone unless you are familiar with the organization.

I personally do not think that you should pay fees to an employment agency that says it will find you a job. My feeling is that an organization that is not willing to pay the employment agency its fees and expects the applicant to pay is an organization to avoid. However, I recognize that some organizations are in need of qualified employees but cannot afford the expense of using an employment agency. I am advising caution as you enter agreements with organizations that promise to find you a job. Unfortunately some of these organizations expect applicants to make a partial payment to them prior to finding you a job opportunity. You should research the history of the organization promising to find you a job and contact their past clients to assess their success in finding employment.

# Job Search/Interview Hints

In searching for ideas to assist job seekers in becoming employed, I found the following suggestions:

- Never disclose anything about your past that you do not have to, but be upfront with direct questions. If the interviewer asks personal questions, keep your answers professional and focused on the job you are interviewing for.

- Never disclose anything about your medical history unless you feel that there are changes in accommodations that need to be made. With blood pressure, this is totally unnecessary.

- Never discuss family, children, etc. If you bring it up, interviewers can ask questions. They are not allowed to ask about your personal information, such as marriage and children, though. If they do say something first, say, "Oh, I didn't think you could ask me those questions."

- Never, ever, ever bring children with you to a job interview…ever.

- Never badmouth your former employer, boss, or supervisor. If you want to be immediately excluded from a job, telling an interviewer how your former boss made you so angry you just walked off the job is the way to go. Otherwise, try to focus on the positives of your previous employer.

– Never discuss lawsuits, etc., brought against former employers. This could label you as a troublemaker.

– Always reveal any criminal background you may have, even a DUI/DWI or spitting on the sidewalk. Too many people do not realize that when a criminal background check is done, even magistrate court counts, and paying a speeding ticket is an admission of guilt.

– Always list previous employers, but not necessarily your supervisor. A close coworker is acceptable as a reference, but put the coworker's title. However, be prepared to answer questions about your working relationship with your supervisor. Try to answer these questions in the most positive way possible. Never criticize your former supervisor, especially by "name-calling."

– Always contact those whom you intend to use as references. Ask them. If they prefer not to be used as a reference, be understanding and do not question their decision. Sometimes people's personal references can be very damaging. Be prepared with names, complete addresses, and phone numbers when you apply.

– Always have a current typed résumé. This makes a big impression. But don't make corrections in pen, etc. I keep mine on a computer so I can easily make any changes.

- Always "overdress" for the interview, but don't go overboard. It is almost never appropriate to wear jeans and a T-shirt to an office-type job interview. Then again, you don't want to wear a suit and tie to an interview for a casual position. But even here, make sure your clothing is clean, pressed, and in good repair. Jeans and a button-down shirt are great. Also, make sure you are clean and well-groomed, no matter what position you are seeking.

- If you have previous positive reviews or evaluations from your employer, bring copies for your application. But be careful if everything is marked "Excellent." That makes me a bit wary. We all have things we need to work on, and although positive reviews are good and show your past history, they don't count with me as much as a job reference does.

- Make sure you have a firm handshake. Nothing turns me off faster than a "cold fish" handshake from someone. But don't overpower the interviewer. If you put the person on his or her knees, you went too far.

- Maintain good eye contact during the interview, but do not "stare down" the interviewer.

- Try to be as relaxed as possible. Don't be afraid to tell the interviewer if you are a "bit nervous," but try not to break out in a cold sweat.

- Be pleasant and smile when appropriate. A smile really does brighten your face and make you look more positive.

Prepare yourself for the following questions:

- Why did you leave your last place of employment?

- Do not place blame here. A good answer is something like, "I feel that I wanted to expand my responsibilities more and I had reached my potential in my position," or "No room for advancement."

- What are your best qualities?

- What are the areas that you feel you need to work on?

- Do not answer "I don't know" to either of the two above. Do not answer anger management to the second question.

- How do you handle conflicts with coworkers? With supervisors?

- How will hiring you benefit XXXXXXX Company?

- Where would you like to see yourself in five years, ten years, etc.?

At the end of the interview, thank the interviewer for his or her time and consideration. Ask when you can expect to hear back, and wish the person a good day.

The web page containing the preceding hints is entitled Job Search/Interview Hints. Here is the address:

http://www.bipolarworld.net/job_school/job_search.htm.

# Job Interview Suggestions

"Stand Out in the Interview," an article on page 19A in the August 14, 2010, edition of *The Dallas Morning News* from the Associated Press, credits the Creative Group of Robert Half International for the following job interview tips:

- Do your prep work – Visit the organization's website, search online for new articles, and ask people in your network if they have any insight about the organization.

- Put your best foot forward from the start – Be polite to the reception staff when you check in, and smile warmly with everyone you meet.

- Be aware of body language – Subtle cues, such as your eye contact, facial expressions, and posture, will affect how hiring managers perceive you.

- Have a good story to tell – Be prepared to provide memorable anecdotes about how you have helped solve business problems. Describe the challenge, talk about your actions, and outline the results. Come with interesting questions.

- Be yourself – A hiring manager wants to get to know a real person whom he or she would be happy to see every morning at the office.

- Stay positive – If you do not get the job, if you accept rejection graciously, you may put yourself first in line for the organization's next opening or if someone decides not to take the offered job.

# Personal Appearance at Interviews

An article on page 1J in the July 10, 2011, issue of *The Dallas Morning News,* "Personal Appearance and Attributes Could be Hurting Your Chances for a Promotion," by Amy Winter of Creators Syndicate, provides some suggestions about job applicants' appearance at interviews. Here are some no-no's:

- No bad breath

- No exposed tattoos

- No wrinkled clothing

- No messy hair

- No casual clothing

- No excess perfume

- No excess makeup

With respect to clothing, when I joined IBM, we were instructed to always wear a suit, white shirt, and tie. Thomas J. Watson, founder of IBM, wore a starched, white shirt, tie, and suit when he was selling meat scales to merchants in upstate New York. He said that a salesman's attire should not detract from his or her message.

During my first days at IBM I noticed someone wearing a blue shirt. I inquired as to why he was allowed to wear a blue shirt. I was told that the individual was at 300 percent of his sales quota!

# Prepare for the Interview

An article on page 1J in the July 3, 2011, issue of *The Dallas Morning News*, "Employee Perks are Beneficial to Companies," by Amy Winter of Creators Syndicate, includes a closing discussion that I think is the important section of the article for job seekers.

"As job seekers get ready for company interviews, they try to learn how to present their best skills and knowledge. But being unprepared can make the interview difficult," the article states. "What is the top mistake that job candidates make during an interview?"

Based on a survey by Accountemps, according to the article, one major mistake is that candidates have little or no information about the company at which they are interviewing. Job seekers should take time to research the company so they can exhibit knowledge of the company's objectives and goals. In addition, the applicants should be prepared to discuss their skills and experience. Further, they should be ready to describe their career plans and goals. Candidates should remember some basics: maintain good eye contact, arrive on time, and exhibit enthusiasm and sincere interest in the company and its opportunities.

# The Potential Impact of Skype for Job Seekers

An article on page 1J in the July 17, 2011, issue of *The Dallas Morning News*, "Skype and the New World of Work," discusses Skype and its possible implications. However, I thought the article did not deal with the possible use by organizations to interview job applicants.

When I was with a consulting company, we conducted technical interviews by telephone with applicants to determine their skills in specific computer languages and systems. This interview was critical because it was the primary basis for the hiring decision. Frankly, I often wondered if we were interviewing the applicant or a friend who actually had the required skills we were seeking.

I think that a Skype interview would certainly improve the validity of the remote interview. Face-to-face communications is the richest method for communicating. In addition, a Skype interview would permit both parties to assess if there was a "fit" between the applicant and job opening and would also save time and money for both parties.

If you have not used Skype or similar technologies, I suggest that you update your Internet communication skills. Skype can be downloaded for free.

# FaceTime Job Interview?

My wife and I recently traded in our iPhone3s for iPhone4s. One of the new features of the iPhone4 is the FaceTime feature. This feature enables a visual connection between owners of iPhone4s and iPads when they are using Wi-Fi sites.

This feature is similar to Skype, which was discussed earlier. I am wondering if job interviewers will begin using this FaceTime feature.

An article on page 1J in the August 21, 2011, issue of *The Dallas Morning News*, "How to Put our Best Voice Forward," by ARAcontent, contains tips for phone interviews. I believe these tips would be helpful to those who are interviewing for a job via FaceTime, Skype, or just the telephone.

Before the phone (or Skype or FaceTime) interview:

- Dress for the occasion.

- Use a landline; a cell phone may drop (maybe not).

- Turn off call waiting; it's annoying. (Be in a quiet, solitary place.)

- Place your résumé in front of you, along with the employment ad (perhaps on a table before you for reference).

- Keep pen, paper, and calculator on hand to take notes. (I'm not so sure about the calculator.)

- During the phone (or Skype or FaceTime) interview:

    1. Ask the interviewer for the correct spelling of his or her name and verify the person's title (if the information is not shown on your screen).

    2. Smile as you speak; the interviewer will hear you and perhaps see you as well.

    3. Stand as you speak; the voice will project better. (I am not sure this is a good idea. You may be more relaxed seated.)

    4. Speak slowly; enunciate words and use proper grammar and don't interrupt. (Always good advice.)

    5. Don't ramble; make your answers brief.

    6. Ask questions; show interest in the job and organization.

    7. Thank the interviewer as you sign off.

    8. After the phone (or Skype of FaceTime) interview, send a note of thanks by e-mail or regular mail with one or two days.

    9. Follow up with a contact within a week if you had no response from the organization.

Hiring organizations are looking for candidates who are comfortable with new technologies. I suggest that you spend time learning and using new technologies.

# SECTION VI –
# TEMPORARY
# STAFFING POSITIONS

Much of my career has been involved in the area of temporary staffing. The organizations where I worked provided computer programmers to augment the project staff for organizations doing systems development and/or systems maintenance. Over the past several years, the strategy of outsourcing and using temporary staffing has become a major area of opportunity for job seekers. Many individuals prefer to focus on specific work assignments rather than become part of an organization's internal operations. Once an assignment is completed, individuals can move to another one, perhaps in another location. Following are my blog postings that provide advice to individuals seeking temporary staffing positions.

# Oil Cleanup Jobs and Other Disasters?

The oil spilled in the Gulf of Mexico is most frightening! The cleanup is going to require a long time and will be expensive.

Unfortunately, there seems to always be disasters occurring such as tornados, floods, forest fires, earthquakes, and the like.  As a job seeker, I suggest that you keep current on such events because there may be a great opportunity for you to apply your skills where they are much needed.

# Suggestions for Holiday Job Hunting

The December 25, 2010, edition of *The Dallas Morning News* on page 25A contains suggestions for holiday job hunting in an article by Diane Stafford of the *Kansas City Star* titled "Now's No Time to Take Holiday from Job Hunting." Here are her suggestions for holiday job hunting:

- Send greeting cards or even e-mails to job-club conveners, headhunters, career counselors, professional association leaders, and executives who have helped you.

- Parties are easy times for networking; dress up and put your best face forward. Be upbeat and discreetly publicize your talents and availability.

- Your relatives could be conduits to a new job. It is a good idea to keep them in the loop.

- Holidays provide many charitable volunteering opportunities. Donate your time; you will feel better about yourself, and you may meet key people with helpful contacts.

In addition, continue to send résumés and cover letters to targeted organizations that are most likely to be hiring.

# How to Make That Temp Job Permanent

An article on page 23A in the November 21, 2009, issue of *The Dallas Morning News,* "How to Make That Temp Job Permanent," by Chip Cutter of the Associated Press, suggests how a seasonal job can become permanent. Here are a few points to consider:

- You should let your boss know that you are interested in a permanent job. The old admonition to salespeople is to ask for the order. You should ask for the job!

- You should make yourself available for additional opportunities such as late-night shifts and weekends.

- You should perform any tasks assigned in an excellent manner by arriving early for work, following your schedule, and not requesting time off unless it is absolutely necessary.

- You should meet and interact with existing employees. Since temporary workers are actually auditioning for a permanent job, supervisors watch to see how you fit in with existing employees.

All organizations typically have modest employee turnover. According to the article, cited organizations hire

20 percent to 30 percent of temporary workers for permanent positions.

So here is a chance for you to be a great worker and win a permanent job!

# Opportunities for Temporary Jobs!

As announced by the Department of Labor and reported in the *Wall Street Journal* and many other media outlets on December 5, 2009, job losses for November 2009 slowed to 11,000; however, temporary jobs increased by 52,400!

Many of these temporary jobs were in the manufacturing, distribution, and information technology industries. As I have suggested previously, temporary jobs are frequently the pathways to permanent employment. I suggest that job seekers focus on these temporary jobs.

You might consider submitting your résumé to organizations specializing in providing temporary labor to industries of your experience and specialization.

# GIGs and Office Ports

Watching and listening to WFAA TV, I heard the news-reader talk about GIGs (temporary work – work projects of any kind) and office ports.

This strategy involves unemployed workers gathering at executive suites to search for short-term assignments. Executive suites, or "office ports," have office equipment, Internet, telephone answering, reproduction, and other office services.

This idea reminds me of labor pools where laborers gather and wait for small business people seeking assistance for the day to drive by and offer work.

One person at the office port profiled in the news segment said that she received as many as three or more assignments in a given day. She is having trouble keeping all the balls in the air. However, she is employed and earning money!

Another advantage of an office port is that job seekers share information about available jobs. Further, frequently an opportunity requires several workers.

The idea here is networking! Becoming involved with groups that have similar skills and interests could possibly result in job lead sharing for all!

# Making a Temporary Stint Stick

An article on page D6 in the February 9, 2010, issue of the *Wall Street Journal*, "Making a Temporary Stint Stick," by Melissa Korn, stated that, "With provisional jobs on the rise, becoming a full-time hire takes some effort."

Jody Miller, chief executive of Business Talent Group, a Los Angeles interim-executive placement firm, says she saw a 50 percent increase in requests for temporary talent in 2009 over 2008.

Examples included in the article described how individuals obtained permanent positions from temporary slots. Keys to their successes were clear: Prove yourself to be a performer, and let the bosses know that you would like to have a permanent job!

I encourage temporary workers to make themselves irreplaceable.

# Getting First Real Job or Any Job!

An article on page 1J in the June 13, 2010, edition of *The Dallas Morning News,* "How to Land Your First Real Job," by Metro Creative Connection, provided ideas for getting your first job or perhaps just for getting a job.

While I do not think these ideas break any new ground, I have listed them below:

- Don't rule out temporary positions. The idea is to earn some money, and temp jobs meet that need and may lead to a permanent position.

- Consider a different job section. You should fish where the fish are biting!

- Continue networking. Whether you have a job or not, you should always be networking and increasing your circle of contacts.

- Be on top of your game. Your résumé should be concise, focused, honest, and error free; you should rehearse responses to typical interview questions; your shoes should be polished and clothes clean and pressed; remove all attaching hardware and cover up body art.

- Don't get discouraged. A positive attitude is very important. Interviewers are very perceptive, and no one needs an unhappy employee.

# Temporary Work Can Be Useful

I have discussed the merits of temporary jobs several times, and the subject is a frequent focus for advisers to job seekers. "Temporary Work Can Be Useful," an article on page 1J in the August 8, 2010, edition of *The Dallas Morning News* by Amy Winter of Creators Syndicate, provided the following myths and facts for job seekers:

MYTH 1: Temporary assignments are mainly clerical or lower skills.

FACT: Today more temporary work positions are available in professional and technical companies.

MYTH 2: Temporary work can't be included on a résumé.

FACT: Temporary work projects need to be put on résumés. Put the staffing firm as your employer and then list your job duties at the different companies.

MYTH 3: Temporary work will interfere with your search for a permanent position.

FACT: Temporary work assignments will most likely improve your job search. Many times, these temporary jobs will turn into full-time positions. Or job candidates will improve their skill set in temp positions while looking for a full-time job.

MYTH 4: Temporary work doesn't pay well.

FACT: Temporary jobs usually pay about the same as salaried full-time positions. For specialized skills, the pay may exceed salaried employees' pay.

MYTH 5: Job candidates will have to pay to work for a staffing firm.

FACT: Usually, reputable staffing firms will not ask job seekers to pay for their services. The fees are paid by the client businesses. You should avoid any staffing or employment firm that requires job seekers to pay their fees.

# Pros and Cons of Survival Jobs

"Weigh the Pros and Cons Before Jumping Into a 'Survival Job,'" an article by Pamela Yip in Section 1 of the August 30, 2010, edition of *The Dallas Morning News*, discussed the move to a survival job after being unemployed for a lengthy period.

A survival job is a "low-end, low-paying job that a displaced job seeker takes on a temporary basis (often as a last resort) to cover living costs, in order to survive and avoid bankruptcy or worse," Randall Hansen, a job search expert in Kettle Falls, Washington, was quoted as saying.

The pros listed in the article include income, productivity, and confidence, while the cons include lower wages, multiple jobs, and limited time for job hunting. It seems to me if one needs money to survive, getting a job is the number one priority! I have said many times, if it is raining any shelter is welcomed!

I am thinking pride is the biggest reason the unemployed will avoid a survival job. This feeling is certainly understandable. Hopefully, potential employers also recognize the situation and deal with individuals seeking survival jobs accordingly.

# Leaving the Workplace Can Help Spark New Talents and a New Career

An article on page R1 in the *Wall Street Journal* on October 25, 2010, "Find Your Inner Artist," by Kelly Green, got me thinking about life beyond full-time jobs.

I know that many of us older folks still do part-time work. I am a teacher at the University of Phoenix. Others may do consulting.

However, more free time can be applied to fulfilling activities. One example is my writing of a blog that hopefully is read by some.

A friend has just published his first novel—a longtime dream. Others devote time and energy to volunteer organizations.

The cited article provided three examples: stock analyst–turned-songwriter, teacher-turned-painter, and clothing rep-turned-collage artist.

# Using Your Own Home Computer for Employment

An article on page 1J in *The Dallas Morning News's* October 31, 2010, edition, "The Benefits of Teleworking," by Metro Creative Connection, discussed the advantages of using the Internet by organizations and employees.

While I do not think that this article broke any new ground, it reminded me that many of us now earn some income by working at home. I teach online classes for the University of Phoenix.

Frequently we see the term *telecommuting*; however, the term *teleworking* is a new one to me.

I believe the terms basically have the same meaning—doing work for pay remotely from an organization's offices.

Anyway, perhaps you job seekers who are proficient in using the Internet should seek such opportunities.

I am thinking that this mode of work may be an avenue for employment for individuals with disabilities and/or individuals living remotely from an organization's operations.

# 'Tis the Season for Holiday Jobs

An article on page 13A in the November 15, 2010, edition of *The Dallas Morning News*, "Start Hunt for Seasonal Jobs," from the *Kansas City Star* and the Associated Press, reminds job seekers that retail stores are staffing up for the holiday season.

According to Challenger, Gray & Christmas, retailers were expected to add 500,000 to 650,000 jobs during the season. The year prior 500,000 jobs were added. The average pay for these jobs was $10.60 per hour.

Here is the message for individuals seeking work during the holiday season:

- Apply in person if you can, presenting a friendly, positive, can-do attitude.

- Have previous experience in the industry.

- Be flexible about the shifts you're willing to work.

- Commit to the entire holiday season, including the post-Christmas rush.

- Show a passion for, knowledge of, or loyalty to the company and its products.

# Home-Based Seasonal Work

An article on page 1J in the October 30, 2011, edition of *The Dallas Morning News*, "Apply Now for Home-Based Seasonal Jobs," by Christine Durst and Michael Haaren of Creators Syndicate, provides the following links to jobs available for seasonal workers:

- http://bit.ly/tEDdC8: 1-800-FLOWERS is looking for home-based agents.

- http://bit.ly/s4TSaz: Arise hires home-based independent contractors for a major tax software company.

- http://bit.ly/qQzzYP: VIPdesk hires home-based agents and concierges as customer service agents to handle its Eddie Bauer account.

- www.aplineacess.com/en/: Alpine Access has 1,000 home-based customer service representatives.

The article provides the following advice to job seekers for home-based seasonal jobs:

- Apply early.

- Be flexible and available.

- Present a positive, can-do attitude.

- Emphasize your customer service skills and experience.

- Be a great performer once you have landed a job!

- The Christmas season is a good time to pursue seasonal job opportunities—either home-based or on-site.

# Seasonal Work and Picking Cherries

When I was posting about seasonal home-based work, I was thinking about an article that I just read about the need for seasonal workers in many areas of U.S. agriculture. Increased action by governments to control illegal workers has resulted in shortages of agricultural workers in many areas within the United States.

I support such action and am wondering, with our high levels of unemployment, why U.S. workers cannot meet these demands. I recognize that the agricultural jobs require skill and experience; however, both can be achieved by U.S. citizens. Perhaps the pay is insufficient to attract workers to temporarily relocate to the work areas. But if the financial losses are significant, perhaps the operators may be willing to pay wages that will attract workers.

My wife and I were in Oregon one August and visited The Dalles, which just completed its annual cherry harvest. A waitress at a restaurant told us that the area was filled with pickers who return every year for the cherry harvest.

I am sure California, Texas, and many other states depend on such migratory labor during critical harvests. Is this shortage of seasonal workers a problem that can be solved or reduced by U.S. workers?

# Summer and Other Jobs!

An article on page 1J in the June 5, 2011, issue of *The Dallas Morning News*, "Tips for Finding a Summer Job," by Creators Syndicate, discussed ideas for students and others for finding employment in the summer.

Here are some of the article's suggestions for developing a persuasive résumé:

- List your accomplishments, including examples of your contributions at other organizations.

- Display your knowledge about the organization's business and industry.

- State your interest in a long-term position.

- Include a cover letter to display your communications skills.

I think that it is very interesting that these suggestions are valid for anyone seeking a summer or permanent position.

Your objective is to get an opportunity to meet the hiring individuals in person so you can present your qualifications and win the job!

# SECTION VII – CAREER TRANSITION

The march of technology results in major changes in organizations and jobs. Further, many individuals grow weary of their present vocations and want to move to a more challenging or fulfilling position. In addition, as individuals retire or depart the military, existing work is left behind and new work must be found. The intent of the blog postings reproduced in this section is to assist individuals with transitioning to new jobs and new opportunities.

# Good News for Older Workers

An article on page 29A of *The Dallas Morning News's* April 25, 2010, issue, "Older Workers Likely to Have Edge as Job Market Rebounds," suggested that older workers are in a good position to get jobs. Older workers may have a great deal of experience in the hiring organization's industry, and therefore they will be fast starters.

Older job seekers should stress their experience and willingness to get tasks done with little or no supervision. In addition, older workers may not have as many family responsibilities as individuals with children.

# Tips for Older Job Hunters

"That Awkward Age – Programs Help Older Job Hunters Clear an Extra Hurdle," an article on page 1D in the July 29, 2010, edition of *The Dallas Morning News*, provided helpful suggestions for job seekers of my vintage.

Following are ways to overcome age discrimination:

- Buy a computer and cell phone, if you do not have them already. Almost all jobs require employees to be able to effectively use these devices. It is time to move beyond faxes.

- Dismiss negative thoughts about age. Stay positive by focusing on your strengths and experience.

- Discussions of medical procedures and recent illness are not helpful.

- Look good so you feel good.

- Stay fit and well-dressed. Confidence shown in a job interview can get you down the road to employment.

- Seek out age-friendly employers.

- Use sites such as retirementjobs.com and those found by performing a Google search using the phrase "job sites for older job seekers."

- Network—online and in person. Linkedin.com, civic organizations such as Senior Source, SCORE, and Rotary, and religious organizations are good sources.

# Is Change Good?

My laptop computer sounded like a thrashing machine and refused to compute. I purchased a new Toshiba Satellite Laptop with Windows 7 installed, requiring me to adjust and deal with the differences.

This change in my life made me think about job seekers and perhaps employees.

Maybe change is good.

If your job-seeking strategy is not working, perhaps you should change your job search strategies.

If you are unhappy with your work, perhaps you should seek another vocation.

# The Power of the Cloud and Internet!

*The Dallas Morning News's* March 6, 2011, edition had an article on page 1J by Christine Durst and Michael Haaren of Creators Syndicate, which discussed how the Internet brings magic like mops or perhaps broomsticks coming to life in *Fantasia*, a Disney movie in which all kinds of crazy, widely unpredictably things happen. I sometimes think that the Internet is magic and perhaps it is. Being in the information systems business almost from the beginning, I am constantly amazed at the information and applications that are available on my iphone4. The cloud is another step in this technological journey.

Perhaps in today's world the cloud will produce change and the unexpected. An article on page 52 in *Bloomberg Business Week's* March 7, 2011, edition by Ashlee Vance discussed the power of the cloud. Everyone seems to have his or her definition of the cloud. Here is a definition of cloud computer provided by Wikipedia:

> "Cloud computing describes computation, software, data access, and storage services that do not require end-user knowledge of the physical location and configuration of the system that delivers the services. Parallels to this concept can be drawn with the electricity grid where end-users consume power resources without any necessary

understanding of the component devices in the grid required to provide the service."

Whatever your concept of the cloud and the Internet, it is clear that they are changing the business world as we have known it. Employees can accomplish much of present-day work in their homes. Data necessary for market analysis will be available almost immediately; consequently, marketing strategies will react on a real-time basis.

So what does this mean to job seekers? It is imperative that they become technically proficient in using the Internet and utilizing online information systems. Here are a few suggestions: You should be proficient with word processors, spreadsheet software, e-mail systems, and Internet search engines. When asked by a job interviewer about your computer skills, you need to be able to respond quickly in a positive manner by citing specific skills that you have.

The future is always in front of us; however, yesterday's future is here today!

# Watson and Jobs?

A thought-provoking commentary on page A19 of the February 17, 2011, edition of the *Wall Street Journal*, "Is Your Job an Endangered Species?" by Andy Kessler, reminded me of my early days at IBM. As systems engineers, we were the change makers converting many manual tasks for punch card machines to perform. Now some fifty years later, many technological labor-replacing innovations are in use, and we are wondering where the jobs have gone.

As an individual interested in technology, I marveled at the contest between the IBM computer named Watson (I assume after Thomas Watson, IBM's founder) and two of the highest money winners on the TV program *Jeopardy!* I can only guess what the future of the use of natural-language machines and how such machines or systems will impact jobs.

The *Wall Street Journal* article listed tellers, phone operators, stockbrokers, stock traders, and librarians as jobs that have been eliminated. In the Dallas area, we can include toll takers, telephone operators and service station attendants. The article asked the question "What jobs will be destroyed next?" and suggested that there are two types of workers: creators and servers. Creators are the ones who drive creativity—write code, design chips, create drugs, and run search engines. Servers service the creators by building homes, providing food, offering advice, and working for governments.

After categorizing types of servers, the article concludes with a position note: "Fortunately, history shows that labor-saving machines haven't decreased overall employment even when they have made jobs obsolete. Ultimately the new jobs always overwhelm the drag from jobs destroyed—if policy makers let it happen."

The unknown is where will these new jobs come from and what will they require of us. I think that education in technology and human relations will be important components needed to meet these new job requirements.

# When You Get Laid Off

An article on page 1J in *The Dallas Morning News* on August 30, 2009, titled "Steps to Take If You Get Laid Off," reminded me of my present job as an adjunct teacher for the University of Phoenix.

While many of my students have full-time jobs, some are unemployed and are increasing their education during their job search.

Another idea is to consider getting an alternative teaching certification (ATC). Many unemployed people have a wealth of actual experience in industry that they could share with elementary and high school students. Both the teachers and the students will benefit. ATC is a possible course of action for those with experience that can lead to teaching positions.

Here is an Internet link to information concerning obtaining an alternative teaching certificate in the state of Texas: http://www.texasteachers.org/?hct=cpc_google_dallasGT_alternative_certification&gclid=CO7f_uGTzJwC-FRghDQodrQh0Hg.

# Executive Errands

A growing part of our population is the category of older adults. Many older adults require some assistance in their daily lives.

I know a very resourceful individual who has an extensive list of clients for which he provides many services. For example, he frequently takes and picks them up at airports. Sometimes he gets their automobiles serviced. Often he takes groups to public events such as parties and baseball and football games. He is also a personal shopper for clients.

I am suggesting that you consider personal services positions. In the condominium where we live, I see people going to apartments or homes and taking care of the residents' pets.

# Service Veterans' Qualities

An article in the October 11, 2009, edition of *The Dallas Morning News* by Amy Winter discussed the job market for service veterans. I recommend that service personnel read the article, in which Winter mentioned several important qualities of service men and women that will assist them in getting civilian jobs. I believe that these qualities, which are listed below, will assist anyone in finding and keeping a job:

- A disciplined approach to work

- An ability to work as part of a team

- Respect and integrity

- Problem-solving skills

- An ability to perform under pressure

- Communication skills

# American Corporate Partners Help Armed Services Transition to Corporate Environment

The following information from *Wikipedia* describes how American Corporate Partners (ACP) assists service personnel in returning to the corporate environment.

You can get additional information about assistance provided by American Corporate Partners by linking to its website: www.acp-usa.org.

American Corporate Partners (ACP) is a nonprofit organization based in New York City dedicated to helping recently separated members of the armed services transition to the corporate environment.

ACP provides current and past military members with mentoring and networking opportunities with employees of America's leading corporations.

As of early 2009, ACP's corporate partners include Campbell Soup, Energy Future Holdings Corporation, General Electric, Home Depot, IBM, MacAndrews & Forbes, Morgan Stanley, News Corporation, PepsiCo, URS Corporation, Verizon, The University of Oklahoma, and The University of Texas System.

Participation in the program is free and available in or near the following cities: Atlanta, Chicago, Cincinnati,

Dallas, Denver, Houston, Los Angeles, New York, Norwalk (Connecticut), Oklahoma City, Philadelphia, Raleigh/Durham, San Antonio, the San Francisco Bay area, Tulsa, and Washington, D.C.

# Erased, Sealed, Blocked

In an article on page A1 in the November 11, 2009, issue of the *Wall Street Journal,* "More Job Seekers Scramble to Erase Their Criminal Past," Douglas Belkin states that job seekers are facing a difficult employment market and background checks reach deeper than ever into their past.

"Though the definition, terminology and methods of expungement vary by state, its general intent is to restore people to the legal status they enjoyed before a brush with the law—often giving them the right to answer 'no' when a prospective employer asked if they've been arrested or convicted. Most felonies, such as sexual assault or armed robberies, can't be removed. But in many states, some lesser crimes can. After a successful appeal, official records may be shredded, erased, sealed or blocked from view by anyone except entities such as police or schools."

I suggest that interested parties who may have had an encounter with the criminal justice system obtain a complete copy of this important article either in print or on the *Wall Street Journal* website: www.wsj.com.

# Coming Out of Retirement Requires Some Work

An article in the suggested many baby boomers are considering returning to the workforce. Many of us are semiretired and actually never completely left the workforce. Nevertheless, below are some suggestions:

- Check with the Social Security Administration to determine how additional income could affect your benefits.

- Research organizations that offer employment to older adults. The names Home Depot and Wal-Mart come to mind.

- Update your résumé to emphasize accomplishments while making sure that it is error free.

- Prepare for the interview by rehearsing with a younger friend, offspring, or spouse.

Is there a job that you always wanted, but the pay was not sufficient to support your lifestyle? Perhaps in retirement you can go after your dream job.

Among the people I know who have returned to work is a man who joined the police reserve after completing police training. He is now riding patrol and making arrests! A former IBM friend is now working at Home Depot helping people with their home projects. He has rejected promotions offered because he enjoys working with customers.

Oh, by the way, I am still teaching MBA students at the University of Phoenix.

# Take Advantage of Layoff to Learn and Grow

As suggested by Cheri Butler, associate director of career development at the University of Texas at Arlington, in an article on page 1J in the December 6, 2009, edition of *The Dallas Morning News,* there are several ways that laid-off workers can effectively spend their time. Here are some ideas suggested in the article:

- Spending more time with family and friends

- Fixing up your home

- Exercising

- Relaxing

- Volunteering

- Going back to school

- Starting your own business

- Traveling

I am not so sure of these ideas, however. When I have been out of a job, I was very uptight and spent day and night seeking employment and worrying, but that is just me.

I do remember, however, spending a great deal of time replacing fence posts in my backyard. Perhaps taking on some diversionary projects is a good idea.

# The STEM Fields Are
# Important in 2010 and Beyond!

An article on page 1J in the January 10, 2010, issue of *The Dallas Morning News*, "Make Yourself Indispensable in the Workplace," by ARAcontent, states, "In fact, the U.S. Department of Labor predicts a growing demand for technological advances will result in a job growth of 22 percent for STEM occupations between 2004 and 2014."

What exactly is STEM? STEM refers to careers in science, technology, engineering, and mathematics.

Schools and universities are focusing their curriculums to develop students who are prepared to meet the needs of high-tech organizations.

This prediction does not mean that there is no place for liberal arts graduates; however, it does mean the graduates with STEM degrees will find an improved job market for their training.

What advice do you recommend for graduating high school students and others who are returning for additional training?

# Culinary Schools – Good News for Diners

I was watching Fox News and viewed a piece about a culinary school.

As you know, many out-of-work people are going back to school to upgrade and/or learn new skills. I interviewed a student who is attending an aviation maintenance school in Dallas.

There are government student loans available, and schools and colleges are very effective in getting such loans funded.

I just want to remind students that these loans must be repaid. You should develop a financial plan to repay these loans out of your earnings, hopefully from a higher-paying job that takes advantage of your new skills and education.

I am looking forward to dining at restaurants staffed by newly educated cooks!

# Trained Job Seekers Enter the Workforce

An article by Karel Holloway on page B1 in the February 21, 2010, issue of *The Dallas Morning News*, "Career Curriculum Gets with Times," discussed how vocational curriculums for high school graduates are changing to keep up with new technologies and job opportunities. Job seekers who are contemplating career changes might consider the following vocational clusters:

- Architecture and Construction: Construction management and interior design

- Arts, A/V Technology, and Communications: Fashion design, graphic design, and illustration

- Education and Training: Ready, set, teach!

- Finance: Banking and financial services

- Health Services: Nursing and Cosmetology

- Information Technology: Digital and interactive media

- Law, Public Safety, Corrections, and Security: Law enforcement and security services

- Manufacturing: Retailing and e-tailing, sports, and entertainment marketing

- Science, Technology, Engineering, and Mathematics: Concepts of engineering and technology, engineering design and presentation

- Transportation, Distribution, and Logistics: Collision repair and refinishing

Since high school graduates will be competing for jobs in the vocational areas listed above, existing job seekers should consider refreshing or upgrading their skills.

Job seekers should be aware of competition for jobs from new entries in the workforce. The result may be a downward pressure on salaries.

# Returning to Work

An article on page 1J in the February 28, 2010, issue of *The Dallas Morning News*, "Tips for Employees Returning to the Workplace," by Amy Winter, discussed problems faced by individuals reentering the workplace after being gone for some time. In order to help with the transition back to the workforce, Robert Hosking of Office Team suggests:

- Learn about the organization's culture.

- Refresh your skills.

- Make a routine.

- Introduce yourself.

- Observe colleagues.

Welcome back to work to those of you who are returning after your sabbatical!

# Moms Returning to Work

The Jobs section beginning on page 1J of the April 18, 2010, issue of *The Dallas Morning News* provided advice primarily for women—specifically, moms returning to work and wardrobe suggestions.

Résumé writing can be a bit tricky if one has been out of the workforce for several years. How do you explain to a potential employer what you have been doing and that now you are ready to return to work?

My advice is the old adage "honesty is the best policy." If you have been in school, raising children, taking care of relatives, and/or doing volunteer work, you should describe your activities.

Further, you need to answer some questions:

1. First, why are you returning to work now?

2. Second, how can you immediately contribute to the hiring organization?

3. Third, why should they hire you?

Hopefully, sincere responses to these questions will position you to compete for job openings.

# Nursing – A Great Opportunity!

An article on page 1J of the May 2, 2010, issue of *The Dallas Morning News,* "Nursing Offers Possibilities," from NewsUSA, discussed career potential in nursing. Here is a key quotation from the article:

"Accelerated nursing programs are good ideas for people who want to do something with the education they already have, or who find that their degrees don't offer as many opportunities as they had hoped," says Andrea Higham, director of the Johnson & Johnson Campaign for Nursing's Future. "These accelerated programs put people on a fast track to becoming a nurse, and the nursing profession also benefits by attracting more individuals with diverse backgrounds."

# Are Your Skills Obsolete?

An article on page 33A in the May 16, 2010, edition of *The Dallas Morning News* by Catherine Rampell of *The New York Times* described a woman who lost her job after thirty years of doing administrative work.

Rampell argued that a number of factors were at work here. First, during an economic downturn organizations are forced to reduce their staffs. In addition, poor economic conditions give organizations cover for eliminating marginally performing workers. And finally, advances in technology continue to replace humans in business tasks.

The article provided no easy solutions for those unemployed because of one of more of these factors. I think it is important for such workers to understand their situation and develop a plan to upgrade their skills or to learn new skills. As has been said, "denial" is a river in Egypt and does not improve personal situations.

# A Smooth Exit Leaving No Bridges Burned

An article in *The Dallas Morning News's* June 20, 2010, edition, "Discover the Right Way to Leave a Job," on page 1J by Metro Creative Connection, suggested that regardless of the circumstances of a departure from an organization, you should leave the job with dignity and grace.

Recently while serving as a job counselor, I had several clients who had lost their jobs because of failing to report to work as scheduled. They stated they did not realize they were scheduled to work on the days they were no-shows.

So I asked them what type of reference their employers would provide them. I think you and I know the type of reference they would receive.

What lessons are to be learned? Jobs today are difficult to find, and if you have a good one, you must protect it by your continued and consistent outstanding performances.

# Why Not Earn an Associate Degree?

An article in the June 27, 2010, edition of *The Dallas Morning News,* "Why an Associate Degree Could Be a Good Option," by Liz W. Robbins, stated that individuals with an associate degree earn $400 or more per month than individuals with only a high school diploma.

We are fortunate in the United States that many community colleges provide convenient schedules and reasonable tuition. Nursing, radiology, and respiratory therapy are representative of the many occupational opportunities in the health care industry.

I encourage high school graduates to consider attending a community college to enhance their skills and earning power.

# Battling the Blues

"Battling the Blues," an article by Diane Stafford of the *Kansas City Star* on page 2D of the October 6, 2010, edition of *The Dallas Morning News,* stated that counseling and volunteering can help during a long job hunt. From personal experience, I can say that being unemployed is a very stressful time.

Stafford suggested the following steps for discouraged job seekers:

- Recognize your job loss to begin your recovery and face it head-on.

- Seek resources to tackle the problem using counseling and prescription drugs.

- Present yourself as being an energetic, emotionally stable employee.

- Leave the house and volunteer with a nonprofit group.

- Give help to others, which shows a sense of self-worth and helps build personal relationships that could lead to employment opportunities.

I will add that it is very important to stay busy. Use a day planner to schedule your week. Knowing that you have things to do and places to go reduces thoughts of self-pity and sends you into action!

# The Company Men – The Movie

My wife and I went to see the movie *The Company Men* starring Ben Affleck, Chris Cooper, Kevin Costner, Maria Bello, Rosemarie Dewitt, Craig T. Nelson, and Tommy Lee Jones. The movie depicts the interactions of employees and their families who worked for a large organization in the 1990s that laid-off many employees because of the recession.

Having gone through a similar experience myself, we were able to relate to the feelings and frustrations of the characters. Loss of a job is like losing part of your life. Dealing with such a situation is a serious challenge. The movie depicted how an individual with job loss is supported or not supported by his family and friends. The movie ends with good and bad news, but it is very intense and worth your time.

For those of you weary of job seeking, perhaps the movie will let you know that your emotions are shared by many in similar situations. I think that the support of family and friends is critical to your being able to deal with the circumstances and hopefully lead to a happy ending.

# Being Successful!

An article on page 1J in *The Dallas Morning News* on February 6, 2011, "Tap Your Strengths and Experience When Changing Careers," by Metro Creative Connection, provided suggestions to job seekers hoping to change their careers.

The article, quoting The Conference Board, stated that 61 percent of workers under twenty-five are unhappy with their jobs and that less than 45 percent of workers ages forty-five to fifty-four are satisfied with their jobs.

I remember when I was in high school, someone asked me what I wanted be. I said that I wanted to be a success. Some fifty-six or so years later, I still think that being successful is a worthy ambition. "Happiness is a state of mind or feeling characterized by contentment, love, satisfaction, pleasure, or joy," according to the Cambridge Advanced Learner's Dictionary. Perhaps we spend too much time seeking happiness and not enough time becoming successful.

I discuss elsewhere in this book ideas for changing careers or vocations.

# Should You Change the Focus of Your Job Search from Professional Jobs to Trade and Craft Jobs?

An article by Brendan Case on the front page of the January 16, 2011, issue of *The Dallas Morning News,* "Longtime Workers Struggle with Long-term Joblessness," described a number of situations in which professionals have been laid off from relatively highly compensated jobs after years of service to an organization. These situations are heartbreaking, and these individuals are having a difficult time replacing their income with similar positions.

I am thinking that perhaps these individuals should consider moving from seeking professional employment to seeking trade and craft base positions. For example, I found this ad with only a cursory search using Google: *Schneider has 2000 immediate openings for Over-the-Road drivers in multiple areas of the country.*

I recognize that changing careers and vocations is not easy; however, when it is rainy and stormy, perhaps you should not spend a great deal of time seeking a specific type of shelter.

# Where Will an MBA Take Me?

A special N section in the March 27, 2011, edition of *The Dallas Morning News* had an article by Jane Hill titled "Where Will an MBA Take Me?" that was very encouraging to MBA students and graduates. The article stated, "A recent survey supports what many have suspected for a while—attaining an executive MBA (EMBA) greatly improves prospects for winning a salary increase or promotion."

As a teacher of MBA students, I am convinced that the thinking, writing, and presentation skills developed in graduate business classes are very helpful. Further, as a night-school student and teacher for fifty years, I can state that continuing one's education can be directly related to success in business.

So I suggest that you pursue additional education and always stay current on what is happening. One of my favorite clichés is that there are three types of people in the world:

- Some make things happen!

- Some watch things happen!

- And some ask: What happened?

# SECTION VIII – ENTREPRENEURSHIP AND SCORE

I think that many individuals dream of one day owning and operating a business. I have opened and operated three different businesses; however, I am not in the class of Bill Gates, Michael Dell, or more recently Mark Zuckerberg. I can state that being an owner and depending on it for your livelihood is challenging and daunting. I hope that the following compilation of blog postings will provide some assistance and comfort to individuals striking out on their own.

SCORE is a volunteer organization affiliated with and sponsored by the U.S. Small Business Administration. SCORE is staffed by individuals who have had business careers and are eager to share their experiences to assist others in forming businesses.

# Doing What You Love?

An article on page 1J in the October 2, 2011, issue of *The Dallas Morning News*, "Is 'Doing What You Love' Good Advice?" provided an example of an out-of-work person who had a hobby of building wooden outhouses. The person, after several false starts, drew over a million viewers and $100,000 of ad revenue from a YouTube posting.

I am sure there are many examples of hobbyists who have converted their passions into moneymaking endeavors. Probably there are even more examples of individuals who have tried and failed to make a commercial go of their hobbies. So what is the message from this idea?

I think that if you have a passion for a craft, musical talent, or technical skill, perhaps you should try to leverage it into a moneymaking enterprise or job. If you dream of success, you will never achieve it if you do not take risk.

The Internet has proved to be fertile ground for planting seeds of innovation. Who knows, you may be able to reap an abundant harvest of your hobby or passion. I hope this metaphor encourages you to action!

# Working at Home and/or at the Office

An article on page 1J in the September 20, 2009, issue of *The Dallas Morning News,* "The Ups and Downs of Working from Home," by Metro Creative Connection, discussed the pros and cons of working from your home. As an online faculty member at the University of Phoenix, I have been working from my home for almost ten years.

Here are the pros the article identified in the article:

- You can spend time with the kids.

- You can dress down every day.

- You can better manage your time.

- You have more flexible time.

- You'll save money.

Here are some cons that I thought of:

- Your pay may not be as good.

- You may get cabin fever.

- You miss see and speaking with people face to face.

- Who will you have lunch with?

Many jobs in today's environment have telecommuting components. Frequently, a weekly work schedule includes time at the office as well as time in the home office. If one is paid by the hour, online systems are very effective at recording time worked.

On the other hand, if you are paid by the delivery of defined services and products, then payment is based on the timely delivery of such products or services. As an online teacher, I have flexibility as to when I do my work; however, I must be attentive to my students on a daily basis. If I am absent for three days from my online class, the school will come looking for me.

# Thought About Driving a Truck?

My wife and I took a trip to Atlanta on I-20 and returned to Dallas via Nashville, Memphis, and Little Rock on I-30. Hundreds of trucks but only one Greyhound bus were on the road.

A client at SCORE is a career truck driver investigating starting his own trucking business. He told me that he earns about a dollar per mile driving his truck. He typically drives six days a week, averaging about 500 miles per day. He said that his monthly income averages about $12,000.

If you are unemployed, I suggest that you consider driving a truck. I frequently hear ads on the radio and see ads in publications for drivers.

# Independent Contractor or Employee?
# Some Clarification

As discussed in an article on page 8 of the fall 2009 issue of *Texas Business Today* by William T. Simmons, legal counsel to Texas Workforce Commission Chairman Tom Paulson, *contract labor* is a very misunderstood term.

Is a worker an independent contractor, or is a worker an employee of an organization? The article lists the following three criteria to be considered an independent (some states require only two criteria to be met):

- The worker is free from control or direction in the performance of the work.

- The work is done outside the usual course of the company's business and is done off the premises of the business.

- The worker is customarily engaged in an independent trade, occupation, profession, or business.

Frequently, temporary help personnel are employees of a staffing organization and are not independent contractors. Nevertheless, "An independent contractor is self-employed, bears responsibility for his or her own taxes and expenses, and is not subject to an employer's direction and control. The distinction depends upon much more than what the parties call themselves."

I suggest that job seekers review the Internal Revenue Service requirements to become an independent contractor before assuming that role.

# Put Up Your Own Shingle!

Many articles, as well as postings in my blog, deal with temporary jobs and consulting positions. Since organizations are reluctant to hire permanent employees because of economic and governmental uncertainly, the demand for short-term workers has increased as organizations' need for additional personnel has increased.

Several years ago when I was unemployed and looking for work, I decided to open my own business. While I am not Bill Gates or Michael Dell, I was relatively successful with my own small business. Consequently, I encourage job seekers with an entrepreneurial spirit and drive to consider putting up his or her shingle!

As a volunteer with SCORE – Counselors to Small Business, I have opportunities to meet with clients who dream of opening their own business. The three basic strategies to follow when your objective is to open a business are:

- Buy an existing business.
- Buy a franchise.
- Start your own business from scratch.

Space does not permit a detailed discussion of these options; however, a SCORE counselor will be pleased to provide assistance at no cost. If you are considering opening your own business, I suggest that you review the information on the SCORE website: www.score.org.

# How to Succeed in the Age of Going Solo!

An article on page R1 in the February 8, 2010, edition of the *Wall Street Journal*, "How to Succeed in the Age of Going Solo," by Richard Greenwald, was very informative for individuals working as consultants or freelancers. Here are some of the key points discussed:

- Think long term – You may be on your own for a long time—prepare for a marathon, not a sprint: Get your own business cards, launch a website, get a business cell phone, establish a home office, or rent an executive suite.

- Pick the right skills and keep them fresh – For technical skills and expertise that are too expensive and too infrequently used, you should attend workshops and training courses at community colleges.

- Join a network – Most successful consultants are in a network or community of consultants.

- Have your own space – Home activities and family sounds do not lend themselves to a professional environment—consider renting or sharing an executive suite.

- Think like an entrepreneur – Develop a business plan including mission, measurable objectives, and strategies to accomplish the objectives.

Since many organizations need more employees but do not want long-term labor commitments, there is an increased demand for temporary workers and consultants.

# Positive Hiring Signs – Real Estate Opportunities!

The media—radio, TV, and print—are filled with positive signs about an improving employment picture. I hope these signs have resulted in job opportunities for readers.

With so many homes being foreclosed and then hopefully resold, I think there are opportunities for employment in real estate. Two of my friends are now studying to pass a real estate exam and are planning to become real estate agents.

Many foreclosed homes need repair prior to being listed for resale. Consequently, there have to be improving opportunities for individuals with construction experience seeking employment. You might visit Lowe's and Home Depot stores to check on employment opportunities.

I frequently encourage job seekers to read notices located in the areas of the stores where contractors and builders come to purchase materials and to network with store employees who sell to contractors, landscapers, and handy-people (handymen may not be politically correct).

# Self-Employment Could Be the Answer

An article on page 1J in the October 10, 2010, edition of *The Dallas Morning News*, "Self-Employment Can Help Fuel Recovery," by North American Precis Syndicate, stressed the importance of self-employment to the U.S. economy.

As a SCORE counselor to small business, I have opportunities to assist many individuals who have or plan to begin their own business. Typically such individuals are energetic, creative, and risk takers. Unfortunately many lack adequate financial resources to start a small business.

There are three basic approaches to becoming self-employed or opening a small business:

- Start from scratch.
- Buy a franchise.
- Buy an existing business.

If you have special skills in fields such as information systems, engineering, and health care, you might consider becoming an independent contractor or a contract employee.

Regardless of the approach taken, getting busy with a potential income-producing activity is much better than remaining at home hoping for lightning to strike!

Please review the tools available for small businesses at www.score.org.

# Home-Based Work Websites

"Supplement Your Income with Home-Based Work," an article by Christine Durst and Michael Haaren of Creators Syndicate on page 1J of the December 5, 2010, edition of *The Dallas Morning News*, suggests work you can do at home using the Internet. There are many such home-based opportunities posted on the Internet that can be found using Google or other search engines.

One such service is Work-from-Home-Free Match Up Services at http://homeincomelocator.com.

While I cannot personally recommend any of these sites, they are ones the article suggests:

- Ejury.com; jurytest.com: Attorneys use the Internet to try cases using virtual mock juries. You might be able to earn five to fifty dollars for rendering your verdict.

- UserTesting.com; Userlytics.com: Site testers can earn money by answering questions concerning sites under construction.

- Ticketpuller.com: You can be paid for going online and purchasing hard-to-obtain tickets for concerts, sporting events, and the like.

- Chacha.com and KGB.com: Home-based researchers can get paid for fast responses to questions. I am told such sites may be helpful to students.

- Focusfwdonline.com and 2020research.com: How about joining an online focus group?

- MTurk.com: You can get paid for identifying objects in photos or videos, transcribing audio, or giving personal opinions.

# You Can Become a Virtual Assistant (VA)!

*Bells Are Ringing*, a musical that opened on the stage in 1956 and was made into a motion picture in 1960, depicts an answering service for organizations and individuals. I thought of this answering service that found itself in financial problems when I read about a virtual assistant in the January 23, 2011, edition of *The Dallas Morning News* on page 1J.

I remember in *Bells Are Ringing* that booking bets was a major service. The *Morning News* article, by Christine Durst and Michael Haaren of Creators Syndicate, suggested that "virtual assistants" should provide their services to small businesses and sole professionals using e-mail, telephone, courier, and the Internet. The article suggested that VAs provide word processing, transcription service, daily schedules, correspondence, concierge services, social networking, and perhaps order taking (not bets).

While the cost of establishing a VA home-based business can be less than $1,000, the article provided these admonitions:

- Do the necessary self-assessment – Operating your own business is not like being an employee. You are your own boss and have to actually run a business rather than taking orders from a supervisor.

- Make sure your family is on board – Working at home means working, not just being a dad or mom and watching TV.

You need to be prepared to market your business – My experience in sales is that you have to market your products and services. Waiting for someone to call in an order may be a long and lonely wait.

# Consider Being a
# Personal Virtual Assistant

An article on page 1J in *The Dallas Morning News's* January 15, 2012, edition, "A Virtual Way to Assist Employer," by Christine Durst and Michael Haaren of Creators Syndicate, answered a reader's question about opening a home-based business. The reader had ten years of experience as an administrative assistant.

Using the acronym PVA (personal virtual assistant), the writers suggested that executive-level personnel typically have a great need for someone to handle many scheduling and personal tasks. Further, the authors made the point that an independent contractor removes the requirements for payroll taxes and benefits that accrue to an organization's employees.

In addition, our organizational culture seems to have removed "girl Fridays" from the workforce. Have you asked someone to pick up your cleaning or bring you coffee lately?

The PVA industry originated in the early 1990s in countries such as India, the Philippines, and Australia. However, the field is just beginning in the United States.

If you enjoy taking care of details and errands for others, I suggest you consider becoming a PVA.

# Noncompetition Agreements

In the *Texas Business Today* winter 2011 edition, published by the Texas Workforce Commission, an article on page 10 by Marissa Marquez, legal counsel for Chairman Tom Pauken, discussed noncompetition agreements. Organizations use such agreements to protect their proprietorship of information and relationships with customers and employees. When employees or contractors leave an organization, how can the organization keep the departing individuals from immediately selling to the organization's customers or contacting and hiring away its employees?

While operating a consulting company, I insisted that my employees and contractors sign noncompetition and confidentiality agreements. Typically such agreements prohibited the departing individual from marketing to my customers or soliciting to hire my employees for a specific period.

The question often posed is: Are noncompetition agreements enforceable? As the article states, the answer is it depends. Marquez wrote that the Texas Legislature in 1989 enacted section 15.50(a) of the Texas Business & Commerce Code, which states the requirements that make a noncompetition agreement enforceable.

The issue is most complex and lawyers should be consulted, and the following requirements must be met:

- Ancillary to an otherwise enforceable agreement: The employee's promise not to compete must be a part of a related or underlying contract imposing obligations on both the employee and employer.

- Reasonable time limitations: The code requires the noncompetition agreement to contain a reasonable time limitation as to how long the employee is restrained from competing. In some cases courts have held that two–five years is reasonable. However, the time limitation may be dependent on many factors, including the position previously held by an employee and the factors involved in the departure.

- Reasonable geographical limitations: Here again every case or situation may be different. The test must be reasonable. If an organization does business in only one city, an individual could not be restricted from doing business in another city.

My advice to job seekers is that you review carefully an employment agreement before signing. I understand that getting employed is paramount and that you may have to hold your nose as you sign and get to work!

# Jump-Start Your Entrepreneurship

*The Dallas Morning News's* March 20, 2011, edition had an article on page 1J by Christine Durst and Michael Haaren of Creators Syndicate, "Jump-Start Your Entrepreneurship Engine." The article stated that many employment experts are urging individuals to consider entrepreneurship in their career planning. The article pointed out that numerous companies are gradually shifting toward an independent-contractor workforce and away from employees. Our nation in the old days, before the Industrial Revolution, was a nation of entrepreneurs such as farmers, cowboys, blacksmiths, shopkeepers, fisherman, undertakers, and so on.

I suppose the many unknowns, including employment legal requirements, the uncertain economic times, and the cost of capital, are reasons why employers are reluctant to hire additional employees. As previous owner of a contract computer programming business, I can appreciate how attractive independent contractors can be to an organization.

However, before becoming an independent contractor or entrepreneur with your own business, you should do your homework. As a SCORE counselor, I frequently counsel with individuals contemplating opening their own business or becoming an independent contractor. It is most important that an individual plan to operate a business for three–six months before it will generate sustainable income. Further, he or she must have a comprehensive business plan that includes financial and sales projections.

Before starting out on your own, I suggest that you visit SCORE's website, www.score.org, and make an appointment with a counselor. The advice and assistance that you receive will cost you only time, and it may be the most valuable time you will ever spend.

# Working-at-Home Websites

An article on page on 1J in the May 29, 2011, issue of *The Dallas Morning News*, "Home-Based Agents in Demand," by Christine Durst and Michael Haaren of Creators Syndicate, discussed organizations that seek home-based call center agents. The article suggested that such jobs typically pay between nine and twenty dollars per hour. However, it is important to note that many costs, such as transportation and wardrobe, are eliminated. Some organizations also offer medical and retirement benefits.

Cultural problems resulting from call centers located offshore, such as in India, encouraged organizations to seek home-based agents who are U.S. citizens. Here are some websites contained in the article that may provide job seekers avenues for finding home-based employment:

www.uloop.com – Uloop is a Student Powered Market Place.

www.cloud10corp.com – A Transcom Company

www.arise.com - Arise Virtual Solutions Inc.

www.vipdesk.com -  VIPdesk

www.hirepoint.com/athome - TeleTech

These sites were current as of publication; however, since sites frequently change, they may not be active when you link to them.

# Suggestions for a Home-Based Business

An article on page 1J in the May 1, 2011, issue of *The Dallas Morning News*, "How to Wreck a Home-Based Business," by Christine Durst and Michael Haaren of Creators Syndicate, provided the following advice on what to avoid when planning a home-based business:

- Don't forget about your family. You should not neglect your home chores and responsibilities, such as running errands, car pools, garbage removal, and food shopping.

- Make sure that you have the agreement and support of your family before embarking on a home-based start-up.

- If you have a website, maintain and update it frequently. Websites that are neglected can become stale. Provide information and images that will encourage individuals to frequent your site.

- Watch your expenditures! It is fun to purchase new office and computing equipment, sign on to expensive monthly Internet services, and develop expensive marketing materials. The larger your monthly expenses, the longer it will take to develop a break-even or profitable business.

- Be aware of naysayers who may discourage your plans and induce guilt, regret, discouragement, cynicism, and disapproval.

- Focus your home-based business on something you care and know about, not the latest craze such as late-night TV merchandise.

- Make use of your own experience and interests.

My first home-based business was providing computer programmers on an hourly basis to medium-size organizations. I found the work challenging and somewhat profitable.

# More Discussions Focused on Home-Based Businesses' Websites

An article on page 1J in *The Dallas Morning News's* November 27, 2011, edition, "Six Unusual Home-Based Businesses," provided the following examples of home-based businesses:

- Bottled art: Laura Bergman turns pieces of broken glass into homemade jewelry. www.bottledupdesigns.com

- Shop fashionably: Alexandra Suzanne Greenawalt, a freelance personal stylist and fashion expert based in New York City, takes clients out shopping or advises them "in their closet." www.alexandra-stylist.com

- All about cats: Lynn Maria Thompson's business, Old Maid Cat Lady, offers products for cats and people who love cats. www.oldmaidcatlady.com

- Invisible writer: Judy Katz is an experienced ghostwriter. She has ghostwritten or edited over twenty-two books. www.ghostbooksters.com

- That's the shot: Steven Holtzman and his father have been running West Coast Aerial Photography Inc. from a home office since 2001. www.photopilot.com/blog

The article states that the above list is just a sampling of hundreds of specialties that are Internet home-based businesses. You can review more examples of home-based businesses, including open jobs, at Rat Racer Rebellion. www.ratracerebellion.com

# Make a Job of Your Avocation!

An article on page 1J in *The Dallas Morning News's* November 20, 2011, edition, "It's Never Too Late to Follow Your Dream," by Lindsey Novak of Creators Syndicate, suggests that it is never too late to pursue your dream job.

The article quotes a reader as saying that friends advise that changing careers late in life is a big mistake, and with this economy people should be satisfied with the job they have.

The article got me thinking about avocations. When talking with my students or clients, I suggest that if they are bored with their present job and are not giving it their best efforts, they should consider spending time with their dream job or hobby or starting a small business. Energy not being used can be redirected to challenging tasks that are very satisfying. Who knows? Maybe your performance on your current job will be improved!

I am a retired computer person, but I continue to teach at the University of Phoenix and do volunteer work at SCORE and the North Dallas Shared Ministries. Maybe this book will eventually make me a millionaire!

# SECTION IX –
# CONDUCT AT WORK

Your reputation is the key in finding employment. Hiring companies will ask about your experience and background. In addition, they will check your references and ask individuals who know you about your performance and character. Your work record will always be with you, so it is important to always be a positive performer. Here are some blog postings that may reinforce the importance of your work history.

# Stress and Struggling

As anyone who reads my blog knows, I am really fond of lists. Writers use lists to summarize their main ideas. My strategic management students analyze organizations by identifying lists of strengths, weaknesses, opportunities, and threats. So I was really drawn to "Keep Stress at Bay during Job Hunt," an article directed to job seekers on page 1J in *The Dallas Morning News* on November 21, 2010, that contained a helpful list.

A question was raised by a job seeker to article author Cheri Butler: "The job-search process has left me stressed. Any tips on what I can do to better manage the uncertainty?" Cheri's answer: "The job-search process can be challenging and exhausting and often creates stress and anxiety for the job seeker. Here are some summarized suggestions for de-stressing:"

1. Find time for yourself. Put time on your calendar to do relaxing and fun things.

2. Find time to help others. Volunteer in your community using your particular skills.

3. Find time to exercise. Exercise creates the release of endorphins, which have been proved to combat depression and to produce healthy results such as weight loss and fitness.

4. Find time for family and friends. Make sure you maintain your network of people who will help you to remain positive during your job search.

5. Find time to network with others in the job search. There are many search networks in local areas.

# Signs of Stress

The "Stress and Struggling" blog posting discussed ways individuals can deal with stress. From another perspective, an article on page 1J in the November 28, 2010, edition of *The Dallas Morning News*, "Coworkers' Behavior," by Amy Winter of Creators Syndicate, discussed behaviors that even hardworking employees may exhibit if they are under extreme stress.

These warning signs may indicate that an individual is under stress and needs assistance:

- Extreme tardiness and absences: A dedicated worker starts making excuses to leave the office early or vacates without permission.

- More supervision: Usually, a worker requires less supervision as he or she becomes more familiar with tasks. If an employee suddenly seeks increased attention, it could be a cry for help.

- Decrease in productivity: An efficient worker has an unexpected drop in performance.

- Strained working relationships: A worker starts to become disruptive with coworkers.

- Unable to concentrate: A worker is most likely worried about something else.

- Changes in health or hygiene: A worker starts to pay less attention to his or her appearance and well-being.

- Substance abuse: A worker is probably using drugs or alcohol to cope with stress.

If you observe someone exhibiting any of the preceding signs or perhaps see yourself exhibiting such signs, it is time to provide or receive help. As a manager or peer, it may be difficult to confront the employee directly, so I suggest you contact your organization's human resources department or the employee assistant representative.

Having personally been in an extremely stressful situation, I know how such situations can become very dangerous.

# 2011 New Year's Resolutions

The key objective once you have found a job is to keep it! An article in the January 9, 2011, issue of *The Dallas Morning News* by Amy Winter of Creators Syndicate quoted John Challenger of Challenger, Gray, & Christmas, who suggests the following tips for workers hoping to keep their jobs in 2011:

- Look for more responsibility. Take on challenging duties and keep a take-charge attitude.

- Become part of a company committee. Build new relationships by being more involved in the company.

- Find and/or become a mentor. Serving as a mentor or having one can help develop and achieve workplace goals.

- Look for opportunities to save money. Seek out options that will increase efficiency while reducing cost for your company.

- Focus on mastering a topic in your field. You want to be the "go-to" person for a certain subject at the office.

I think these suggestions could provide answers to an interviewer who asks how you would be an asset to the organization.

# Ways to Keep Your Job

In the summer 2009 issue of *Texas Business Today,* the article "Ten—No, Make That 15—Ways to Keep Your Job," William T. Simmons, legal counsel to Tom Pauken, chairman of the Texas Workforce Commission, outlines steps an employee should take to keep his or her job. I think that the article's "15 Commandments of Keeping Your Job" are instructive not only for employees but also job seekers. I have summarized these commandments:

- Be on time, whether it involves showing up for work, returning from breaks, going to meetings, or turning in assignments.

- Call your manager if you know you will be tardy or absent.

- Try your best: Always finish an assignment, no matter how much you would rather be doing something else.

- Anticipate problems and needs of management.

- Show a positive attitude.

- Avoid backstabbing, office gossip, and spreading rumors.

- Follow the rules.

- Look for opportunities to serve customers and help coworkers.

- Avoid the impulse to criticize your boss or the company.

- Volunteer for training and new assignments.

- Avoid the temptation to criticize your company, coworkers, or customers on the Internet.

- Be a good team member.

- Try to avoid ever saying "that's not my job."

- Show pride in yourself.

- Distinguish yourself.

I suggest that all readers consider adhering to this list of commandants in their work environments.

# Playing Hooky

An article on page 1J in the November 15, 2009, issue of *The Dallas Morning News,* "Economy not Helping Absenteeism," by Amy Winter, suggests that workers have no shame about coming up with unique lies for missing work.

Here are a few creative examples of excuses:

- I got sunburned at a nude beach and can't wear clothes.

- I woke up in Canada.

- Someone threw poison ivy in my face and now I have a rash.

- I was injured catching a seagull.

- I accidentally hit a nun with my motorcycle.

- I got caught selling an alligator.

- I broke my tooth while eating a taco.

- I have a headache from eating hot peppers.

- A bee flew in my mouth.

- My mom said I was not allowed to go to work today.

# *Up in the Air*

My wife and I just attended a showing of the movie *Up in the Air,* starring George Clooney as Ryan Bingham, a corporate specialist whose job is to visit downsizing organizations and inform employees that they are being laid off. Perhaps you can relate to employees receiving the bad news. I certainly can.

The movie graphically shows the emotions of employees as they are told that their services are no longer needed and they are presented with a severance package. How does one cope with such a sudden and traumatic event?

In a scene early in the film, Bingham convinces a recipient of the bad news that his layoff provides him an opportunity to pursue his personal goals, which have been deferred because of the demands of his job. Poignant moments toward the end of the movie show laid-off employees realizing that their situation is not hopeless and that they have the support of their families.

I think the film's message can be encouraging to the many who have been victims of a job loss. I encourage all job seekers to avoid feelings of failure and depression. Remember your strengths and the individuals who support you, and get on with the rest of your life!

# Trends for 2010

*The Dallas Morning News,* in an article on page 1J in its January 10, 2010, issue, "Make Yourself Indispensable in the Workplace," listed the following trends that companies hoped to bring in 2010:

- Strengthening the workforce—employers hope to replace their lower-performing employees with higher performers.

- Focusing more on social media to improve a company's brand

- Bringing back laid-off employees and trainees

- Reducing benefits and perks

- Providing flexible work schedules including telecommuting, job sharing, and compressed workweeks

- Finding freelance and contract workers

- Adding green jobs

- Hiring bilingual workers

- Decreasing business travel

After reviewing the preceding list, what job-seeking strategies come to mind? If nothing comes to mind, then perhaps you should rethink your strategy.

# Busy Working Moms – A Balancing Act

"Busy Working Moms – A Balancing Act," an article on page 1J of the May 30, 2010, edition of *The Dallas Morning News*, by Amy Winter writing for Creators Syndicate, discussed the many roles played by working moms. Winter stated that as companies eliminate positions in order to save money, many working moms are taking on more responsibilities. "Longer work days and increased workloads take away time with kids," the article noted.

The article quoted Mary Delaney of CareerBuilder as saying, "What we're seeing from these moms is a great deal of resourcefulness and resilience as they provide for their families."

Here are some suggestions for working moms by Delaney:

- Interact with other working moms – A support network is a great asset.

- Investigate flexible working options – Such schedules should not impact careers.

- Make a schedule – A plan can budget your time efficiently.

- Use family time – Time with children should take priority over e-mails.

- Plan to have "me time" – Some personal time is important to moms.

# Tips for New and Experienced Workers!

An article in the July 4, 2010, edition of *The Dallas Morning News,* "Tips for College Grads Entering the Real World," by Amy Winter of Creators Syndicate, provided some tips for new workers. However, I think these tips are good advice to all workers.

Here is a summary of the tips:

- Don't trust everyone – Be careful of sharing intimate details with coworkers.

- Avoid office gossip – Steer clear of being the busybody, comedian, or matchmaker.

- Prove your ability – Walk the walk instead of talking the talk. Demonstrate your value and worth.

- Remember, time is money – Avoid writing wordy e-mails and spending too much time chatting.

- Maintain job safety – Become independent and dependable.

- Show respect – Treat everyone with respect, courtesy, and dignity.

- Keep bad attitudes at bay – Maintain a positive attitude at all times.

- Go above and beyond – Perform your job faster and better than your peers.

I believe if you follow these tips, your career will progress, and you will be rewarded.

# Do You Have a Difficult Boss?

An article on page 1J in the July 17, 2011, issue of *The Dallas Morning News*, "Tips to Deal with Difficult Bosses," from Creators Syndicate, discussed five types of difficult bosses.

The article quoted a study by Office Team, a staffing service organization that questioned 441 employees. The survey found that 46 percent of respondents have worked for an unreasonable boss. Among these employees, 35 percent of the employees stayed with the organization and tried to deal with the boss, 24 percent remained with the organization and suffered through distress, and others decided it was time to leave the organization. Further, 27 percent quit when they found another job, and 11 percent could not take it anymore and quit without another job opportunity.

Here are the five types of difficult bosses and suggested coping strategies:

- The micromanager: This type of boss will literally look over your shoulder to make sure the duty is performed to his or her idea of perfection. Strategy: Show your boss that you can be trusted with your assignments by making all deadlines and maintaining an eye for details while keeping the manager updated on your progress.

- The poor communicator: This type of boss doesn't give direction. Deadlines and objectives fail to be communicated clearly. Strategy: When working on an assignment, ask to make sure that you aren't missing any important information. If confused, request clarification.

- The bully: This type of boss wants it only one way. Many times, this boss can be bad-tempered and become easily frustrated. Strategy: You must defend yourself. If you have a suggestion, support your idea with reasoning, but maintain a calm manner. Getting angry will only make the situation worse.

- The saboteur: This type of boss doesn't acknowledge hard work performed by others. Workers are rarely identified for a job well done. This boss will take praise for employees' successes and blame others if they fail. Strategy: Try to display your contributions to upper management.

- The mixed bag: This boss is constantly changing—a friend one day but turns on you the next. Strategy: Try not to be affected by the manager's mood swings. When you detect a manager is in a bad mood, avoid him or her as much as possible.

I think that an important teaching point for managers and aspiring managers is to make sure your management style is not one of these five. As a matter of fact, you should use the opposite approach in managing.

Can you relate to these types of difficult bosses? I can.

# You Landed a Job! What's Next?

An article in the June 26, 2011, issue of *The Dallas Morning News*, "In Recovery Mode," by Eileen Ambrose of the *Baltimore Sun*, provided financial suggestions to individuals who have become employed after a lengthy job search.

First, let me congratulate you on your success in landing a job! Here is a brief summary of Ambrose's suggestions:

- New job, new budget. Put together a new budget as soon as possible that is based on your new income.

- Rebuild cash cushion. You should begin building an emergency fund of three to six months of living expenses.

- Save for retirement. Enroll in the employer's retirement plan by contributing enough to get employer match.

- Pull credit reports. You should get free copies of your credit report by calling 877-322-8228. To restore good credit, repay debt and make sure you consistently pay bills on time.

- Avoid splurging. You should resist the temptation to treat yourself to a big purchase such as a vacation or home renovation. You might reward yourself and your family with more modest outings such as movies and nice dinners.

I think that the most important thing to do when you become reemployed is put all your energies into performing outstandingly in your new job by exhibiting initiative and a positive attitude.

# Conclusions

This compilation of my writings is not the conclusion of the story of the never-ending search for employment. Rather, my blog is a continuing journal of suggestions for individuals seeking employment in order to support themselves and their loved ones.

As long as I am able, I plan to augment the advice and counsel contained in my blog postings.

I encourage all—whether employed, unemployed, or retired—to give support to job seekers by contributing comments, suggestions, and experience to my blog, www.gjbygj.blogspot.com.

The rewards for such efforts will be the satisfaction of knowing that people helping people is a noble goal for all to seek.

# Appendices

## Appendix A – Glyn Jordan Résumés

## Business Résumé

## H. GLYN JORDAN

## BUSINESS SUMMARY

Over fifty years experience in information systems including management, marketing, and systems engineering. Strong operational, entrepreneurial, and people skills with the proven ability to plan and execute software projects, market products/services and manage resources to produce bottom line results.

MOD2000, INC.
* 1994 - 2003 - Founder/CEO
Strategic Staff Services
* 1988 - Present - Founder/President
I. S. International
* 1987 - 1988 - National Sales Director
Systems & Programming Resources, Inc.
* 1985 - 1987 - Regional Manager
Cutler-Williams, Inc.
* 1984 - 1985 - Vice President - National Accounts
* 1983 - 1984 - Vice President - Hospitality Systems
* 1979 - 1983 - Vice President and Regional Manager
Informatics
* 1978 - 1979 - Regional Marketing Manager
IBM Corporation
* 1972 - 1978 - Regional DP Services Marketing
* 1971 - 1972 - Senior Marketing Manager
* 1969 - 1971 - Industry Marketing Specialist
* 1966 - 1968 - Marketing Representative
* 1963 - 1965 - Systems Engineer

Collins Radio Company
* 1962 - 1963 - Marketing Analyst
* 1960 - 1962 - Project Administrator
U.S. Army
- 1960 - 1966 - Captain, S-3, 519th Maintenance Battalion,
- Dallas, Texas
- 1959 - 1960 - 2nd Lieutenant, Active Duty Allied Liaison Officer
- Ft. Belvoir, Virginia

# BUSINESS ACCOMPLISHMENTS

* In association with John Meagher, founded MOD2000 Inc. that specializes in information systems consulting. Major clients include J.C. Penney Direct Marketing Services, Equitable Life Assurance Society, PFL Insurance, EXE Technologies, Protective Life, Fidelity Investments. Initiated an electronic printing consulting practice.

* Established Strategic Staff Services, an information systems and human resources consulting company. Clients included ARKLA, Meridian Oil, Neiman Marcus, ICH Insurance Companies, CASE Methods Development Corp., TK International, Champlin Refining, Partners National Health Plans, and Thiokol.

* Managed SPR branch offices in Dallas, St. Louis, and Tulsa. Region included 50 consultants, 3 sales managers, 2 recruiters, and 3 administrators. Region annual revenues were $4 million and $400,000 profit.

* Directed sales and technical personnel in growth of Southern Region from 25 to 100 consultants at Cutler-Williams.

  − Region produced $5 million revenue and $500,000 profit.
  − Sold and managed the development of a claims processing system generating $4 million.

- Managed Hospitality Systems. The unit provided software maintenance services to 30 hotels.
- Established education offering that provided advanced data processing training.

* Significant IBM Accomplishments:

- Earned nine IBM 100 percent clubs and one IBM system engineering symposium.
- Sold over 20 IBM computer systems and developed consulting revenues exceeding $3.5 million.
- Specialized in insurance, conducted executive seminars, and served as strategy advisor.

# EDUCATION

University of Texas at Dallas – PhD, 1990
Southern Methodist University – MBA, 1962
University of Texas at Austin – BBA, 1959; Beta Gamma Sigma and Sigma Iota Epsilon

# COMMUNITY SERVICE

**North Dallas Shared Ministries – Job Counselor and Interviewer**
**SCORE – Counselors to Small Business – Chapter Chair**
**Highland Park United Methodist Church**

# Academic Résumé

# H. Glyn Jordan

## ACADEMIC SUMMARY

Over fifty years teaching college-level business courses with experience in state and religious-based universities. Extensive experience in both on-ground and online environments.

## ACADEMIC ACCOMPLISHMENTS

2001 to Present – Adjunct Faculty: University of Phoenix – Dallas-Ft. Worth, Houston, and Online Campuses.
Member of initial faculty at this new campus. Facilitating courses in Information Systems, Human Resource Management, Statistics & Research Methods for Managerial Decisions, and Organizational Behavior.

**1991 to 1998 – Professor of Management, Amber University, Garland, Texas.**

**Course concentration: Strategic Management, Human Resource Management, Management Systems, Analysis and Design of Information Systems, and Management Processes & Information Systems.**

**1991 to 1992 – Adjunct Faculty – University of Dallas and The University of Texas at Dallas**

**Lecturer in Strategic Management and International Management, Human Resources Information Systems and Wage and Salary Administration**

**1988 to 1990 Lecturer – TCU and UTA**

**Lecturer in Management Information Systems at Texas Christian University and Lecturer in Social Psychology for the MBA program, The University of Texas at Arlington.**

**1986 to 1990 – Ph.D. Student in Organizational Behavior at UTD**

Subject areas include: Organization Design, Work Behavior, Personnel, Organizational Environment, Social Psychology of Organizations, Interpersonal Dynamics, Information Processing and Interpersonal Skills, Corporate Governance, Research Methodology, Micro and Macro OB Research Seminars, Statistics, Probability, and Econometrics.

1962 to 1975 – Lecturer at SMU Evening Division

Developed and Taught Courses in: Production Control, Industrial Management, and Organizational Behavior and Theory.

1960 to 1962 – Prepared and successfully defended a MBA Masters Thesis entitled "The Development of a Project Schedule and Control System for Research and Development Contracts."

# MAJOR PAPERS/PRESENTATIONS

## *An Empirical Examination of Texas Employment Outplacement Services*

"Downsizing as a Function of Strategic Renewal," Accepted and presented to Texas Conference on Organizations held April, 1990.
"Analysis of Top Companies in Major Groups: 1965-1985"
"Governing Board Sizes of Southwest Universities"
"Linkage of Information Technology (IT) to Changes in U. S. Organizational Culture"
"Move Over Executives and Make Room for the CIO – An Introduction to Management Ecology," Accepted and presented to Texas Conference on Organizations, held April 1988.
"Organizational Topology and Culture as Determinates of Information Richness"
"Stock-Market Value Changes of Top 1000 U.S. Companies Related to Size and Composition of Governing Boards"
"Vector Theory of Destination Decision Making"
"Getting Jobs by Glyn Jordan" – An Internet blog site containing over 200 individual blogs to assist unemployed

# EDUCATION

University of Texas at Dallas – PhD, 1990
Southern Methodist University – MBA, 1962
University of Texas at Austin – BBA, 1959; Beta Gamma Sigma and Sigma Iota Epsilon

# COMMUNITY SERVICE

North Dallas Shared Ministries – Job Counselor and Interviewer
SCORE – Counselors to Small Business – Chapter Chair
Highland Park United Methodist Church

# University of Phoenix Résumé

## Instructor Bio:

# H. Glyn Jordan

I have been an on-ground faculty member of the University of Phoenix, Dallas – Ft. Worth Campus for ten years. Professionally, I have two major interests: information systems and university teaching. After completing my PhD, I accepted a full-time position with Amberton University in Garland. During my seven years at Amberton University, my teaching load included such courses as strategic management, human resource management, management systems, and information systems in business. I have also taught business management graduate and undergraduate classes at TCU, SMU, University of Dallas, and UTD. I hold a BBA degree from The University of Texas in Austin, an MBA from SMU, and a PhD from the University of Texas at Dallas.

Much of my business career was with the IBM Corporation in various marketing positions. After leaving IBM I worked with a number of companies in the professional information services business. After ten years of operation, I have closed my small information systems consulting company that provided employment and contract programming services for mainframe, client server, Internet, and electronic printing.

My family consists of my wife, Ann, who has retired from her position as director of the International Program at the Hockaday School in Dallas; a son; daughter; and most important five grandchildren. My wife and I enjoy travel.

I am a volunteer for SCORE, an SBA organization that mentors to small business, and the North Dallas Share Ministries, which provides assistance to persons in need. Further, I am a collector of many items, including cut glass from the American Brilliance Period. In addition, I am active on eBay! I have a blog that assists individuals find employment: http://gjbygj.blogspot.com.

## SCORE Résumé

**H. Glyn Jordan, PhD**

Over fifty years experience in information systems, including management, sales, marketing, and systems engineering. Companies served include: Collins Radio Company, IBM, Cutler-Williams, and Systems and Programming Resources.

Founded three businesses: J-4 Company, Strategic Staff Services, and MOD_2000 Inc. A career in university teaching at SMU, TCU, University of Texas at Arlington, University of Dallas, University of Texas at Dallas, Amberton University, and presently at the University of Phoenix.

Active in volunteer work at North Dallas Shared Ministries, Highland Park United Methodist Church, and SCORE. Wife, Ann, celebrating our golden wedding anniversary in 2009, son, daughter, and five grandchildren.

University of Texas at Dallas – PhD, 1990

Southern Methodist University – MBA, 1962

University of Texas at Austin – BBA, 1959

Beta Gamma Sigma, Sigma Iota Epsilon, Pi Kappa Alpha

# APPENDIX B — THE BEGINNINGS OF GETTING JOBS BY GLYN JORDAN

Getting Jobs by Glyn Jordan (gjbygj)
August 10, 2009

I am establishing this blog to assist unemployed individuals find employment by:

1. Discussing my personal background in finding employment

2. Encouraging others to share their experiences

3. Interacting with individuals seeking jobs concerning their experiences

The link to "Getting Jobs by Glyn Jordan" is "gjbygj."

Here is some my basic understanding about finding a job:

1. Finding a job is a full-time job.

2. Networking is the number one priority in finding a job.

3. Job-search training is very helpful in a job search.

4. Many organizations are ready to assist your job search.

5. A positive attitude is needed throughout a job search.

I look forward to reading your ideas and comments as we develop this blog.

Thanks!
Glyn

Here are some personal Glyn Jordan experiences:

My first job was with the U.S. Army. I was offered three alternatives for my military career. First, I was offered a regular army commission (RAC), which means that you are selecting the army as a career. If I declined the RAC, I was obligated to serve in the active army for two years or six months. After consultation with my wife-to-be, we decided that six months active duty was enough army for us.

Leaving the army after six months, we returned to Hubbard, Texas, and began a job search. I immediately contacted my fraternity brother, Frank Mikeska (may he rest in peace). He had been employed with Collins Radio in Richardson, Texas, and told me that Collins was hiring. While at Collins Radio Company, I became very interested in computers. Collins sent me to a class in Newport Beach, California, where we learned about the Collins computers. However, there were no computer jobs available for me at Collins.

A close friend of mine and my wife's from UT Austin and Corpus Christi was with IBM at the time, and he got me an initial interview with his manager at IBM. After several interviews and some testing, I was offered and accepted a systems engineer trainee job with IBM and resigned from Collins.

After fifteen years with IBM, I decided to move on and joined an insurance software company in Dallas, Equimatics. A previous sales partner at IBM had joined Equimatics a year earlier and was instrumental in my making this decision. Again, networking was key to finding a new job.

After about five months with Equimatics, a friend called me about a district manager position with an information systems consulting firm in Dallas. I had been seeking a management position for several years, so I went to an interview with the company's president. I regretted leaving an organization that I had just joined; however, I felt that I could not turn down this chance to move into a management position. So I joined Cutler-Williams as a district manager.

My time with Cutler-Williams was a great learning experience for me. Becoming an executive and dealing with all sorts of problems, including being sued, was something else. After many successes and some failures, I found myself at an outplacement organization. The story of my interest in finding jobs starts there.

It was during my years at Cutler-Williams when I got involved with the hospitality industry. I was responsible for the division of the C/W that sold, installed, and maintained computer systems for restaurants and hotels. I found the greatest people in this industry are a close-knit group working many, many hours each week focusing on pleasing their guests. I continue to believe that the hospitality industry provides ample career opportunities, and I encourage job seekers to investigate hotels, restaurants, and resorts for jobs. A wide range of vocations is available. I am sure that it is a coincidence, but my son later became a hospitality executive.

It did not work out at Cutler-Williams. My boss and I came to a parting of ways, and I had my experience with an outplacement organization. Perhaps this experience eventually resulted in my interest in the problems of the unemployed. While at the outplacement organization, I found a job using networking techniques. The organization was Systems and Programming Resources (SPR) of Chicago. This job gave me experience with managing three branch offices and numerous sales and operation problems. However, while at SPR, a combination of politics and a family business resulted in my again seeking employment.

My networking again paid off with a job with a start-up organization founded by executives who had left Electronic Data Systems (EDS). I quickly learned that the organizational cultures of EDS and IBM did not mix well. Here again I was networking.

Having been unsuccessful in my previous two organizations, much to the dismay of my wife, I started my own business, which I named Strategic Staff Services (S-3). I sold my first contract with a natural gas producer and distributor in Shreveport, Louisiana (ARKLA). A side note is that I had returned to the University of Texas at Dallas in the PhD program while I was with SPR. S-3 was successful until ARKLA decided to relocate to Houston and S-3's business declined.

As the song goes, along came John. I had met John at Equimatics, which sold life insurance software systems. John had successfully founded his own company but later closed it. At this time he was working as an independent programmer contractor for J.C. Penney Insurance Company of Plano, Texas. John was aware of Penney's requirement for additional programmers, and we formed MOD_2000 to meet Penney's needs. MOD_2000 was successful for eight or more years. During this time I completed by PhD and became an associate professor of business for Amberton University in Garland, Texas. I held this position for about seven years and then left in order to devote more time to MOD_2000.

The early 2000s were not kind to consulting firms, and as business declined so did MOD_2000. Consequently, I went back to teaching with the University of Phoenix (UOP) when it opened its Dallas campus and have remained with UOP for ten years.

While teaching some classes, I have decided to devote more of my time to enjoying life with my wife, children, and grandchildren. I am active with volunteer work with SCORE and North Dallas Shared Ministries, both of which I have discussed in my blogs. We are very involved in our church, Highland Park United Methodist, and in particular a very active Sunday school class—First Light. In addition, we are "world travelers," having visited all fifty states and all seven continents.

No one knows what the future holds, but I continue to seek a positive lifestyle that will always include time for others.